# *The* Five
## Disciplines
### *of* PLC
# Leaders

## Timothy D. Kanold
Foreword by Richard DuFour

**Solution Tree | Press**

a division of

Solution Tree

555 North Morton Street
Bloomington, IN 47404
800.733.6786 (toll free) / 812.336.7700
FAX: 812.336.7790

email: info@solution-tree.com
solution-tree.com

Visit **go.solution-tree.com/plcbooks** to download handouts and access materials related to this book.

Printed in the United States of America

15 14 13 12 11      1 2 3 4 5

**FSC**
**Mixed Sources**
Product group from well-managed
forests and other controlled sources

Cert no. SW-COC-002283
www.fsc.org
© 1996 Forest Stewardship Council

Library of Congress Cataloging-in-Publication Data

Kanold, Timothy D.
  The five disciplines of PLC leaders / Timothy D. Kanold ; foreword by Richard DuFour.
    p. cm.
  ISBN 978-1-935543-42-8 (perfect bound) -- ISBN 978-1-935543-43-5 (library edition)
  1. Professional learning communities. 2. Teachers--In-service training. 3. Educational
leadership.  I. Title.
  LB1731.K27 2012
  370.71'55--dc23
                                    2011016663

---

**Solution Tree**
Jeffrey C. Jones, CEO & President

**Solution Tree Press**
*President:* Douglas M. Rife
*Publisher:* Robert D. Clouse
*Vice President of Production:* Gretchen Knapp
*Managing Production Editor:* Caroline Wise
*Senior Production Editor:* Risë Koben
*Cover and Text Designer:* Jenn Taylor

This book is dedicated to Dorothy Benoit
My "Aunt Dottie"
Whose light shines bright within me

# Acknowledgments

■ ■ ■ ■ ■

I knew I wanted to be a mathematics teacher when I was fifteen. The influence of my high school geometry teacher, Al Foster, made me want to be part of such a great profession. He jump-started my career and provided my first opportunity to write mathematics textbooks. He was my first leadership mentor. That was thirty years ago.

Along the way, I have been blessed to know many incredible and encouraging people. My wife, Susan, encouraged me to write this book and throughout the demanding writing process served as a loving and supportive critic. She challenged and encouraged me to write with clarity, purpose, and passion. The anchor of my life, Susan has brought so much personal joy to the journey. Our youngest daughter, Anna, gave me the grace of time needed to take on this task. She allowed me to inject my ideas about the disciplines of school leadership into her high school life and routines, without complaint. Jean Willis, my mother-in-law, and Tim McIntyre, my son-in-law, provided a model of humor and wit that kept me laughing along the way.

Our oldest daughter, Jessica, has chosen a career of school leadership as a junior high school assistant principal and mathematics teacher. Jess's guidance and thinking provided the template and ideas for the study guide questions in this book. One of my favorite memories is the summer day we spent on the back porch, designing the study guide and creating an early prototype together. Our son, Adam—a civil engineer—provided insight into the value of the disciplines as he applied some of the early writing to his own leadership work for the organization Engineers Without Borders.

Like you, I have had several teachers, leaders, mentors, and colleagues in my professional life who have had a significant impact on my school leadership journey. Jhone Ebert, Dianne Demille, Zack Munoz, Mona Toncheff, Deborah Gonzalez, Peter Lueck, Jerry Cummins, Shirley Frye, Wendy Weatherwax, Jessica McIntyre, Donna Leak, Steve Wood, Dave Napoleon, Cindy Douglas, Theresa Dunkin, and especially Janis Fine at Loyola University Chicago are school leaders who took the time out of their own lives to read and respond to early drafts—with more hours and kindness than I deserved. Almost all of their recommendations show up somewhere in this book.

I learned how to lead because of the great men and women in the mathematics division of Adlai E. Stevenson HSD 125. For sixteen years, we learned to live, risk, and improve together. Although I cannot list them all, they were a team of men and women who demonstrated incredible courage every day. The mathematics program at Stevenson High School became a lighthouse for the nation because of *them*. Special thanks for giving so much to our cause of professional learning communities (PLCs), and for believing in your ability to make great things happen with our students.

There are several people, some of whom you will read about in this book, who had a profound impact on my leadership growth as well: college professors John Dossey, Larry Spence, and Al Otto; mathematics education leaders and icons Shirley Frye and Iris Carl; coauthors Lee Yunker, Jerry Cummins, Peg Kenney, Lee Stiff, Ron Larson, and Laurie Boswell; teacher colleagues during my early leadership years at Stevenson (who tolerated my digging deep into their work with video- and audiotape and classroom experiments that showcased our mistakes and successes together), Mary Layco, Paul Swan, Linda Ruesch, Mary Conway, Jim McGrath, Ron Urich, Don Vanderwal, Chris Kelly, Cathy Rauch, Dolores Fischer, Scott Oliver, Karen Ostaffe, and Neal Roys; staff members Pat Guillette and Todd Slotten; administrative colleagues and professional friends Wendell Schwartz, Dan Galloway, John Carter, Gwen Zimmerman, Diane Briars, Skip Fennell, Mike Schmoker, Kit Norris, Donna Leak, Linda Fulmore, Patti Smith, and Rita Schaefer; and the members of two great leadership boards, the 2002–2007 Board of Education for Stevenson HSD 125 in Lincolnshire, Illinois, and the 2007–2010 Board of Directors of the National Council of Supervisors of Mathematics.

I have thought a lot about school leadership, and writing those ideas into a book is a humbling experience. Taking the vision of the manuscript and turning it into the reality of this book was due to the patience, guidance, and hard work of some remarkable people. Longtime colleagues Nancy Wagner and Charlene Chaussis, along with Risë Koben at Solution Tree and the deep inspection of editor and new friend Joan Irwin, helped turn the original manuscript into a workable document. Solution Tree leaders Jeff Jones and Douglas Rife embraced and supported the early vision for what this book could become, and Gretchen Knapp, editor extraordinaire, brought the book home with her incredible insight and ability to bring coherence and clarity to the work—a mark of a great editorial leader. Each of these colleagues and friends made my writing so much better and embraced my belief in disciplined school leadership. I thank them.

Finally, I realize the tremendous benefit I received from working every day for sixteen years alongside one of the best and brightest "in-the-field thinkers" and thought leaders on deep and meaningful school leadership and reform. The disciplines of PLC leadership sustainability we will study in this book began with his model for others and with his willingness to envision and teach a new reality for unparalleled school success. Rick DuFour understood the tenets of effective, meaningful, and sustained change long before the rest of us. Much of whatever merit this book may have is due to his diligence and commitment to me over the years as a teacher, leader, colleague, mentor, and friend.

■  ■  ■  ■  ■

Solution Tree Press would like to thank the following reviewers:

Scott Carr
Principal, Liberty Junior High School
Liberty, Missouri

Gordon Donaldson
Professor, Department of Educational Leadership
University of Maine
Orono, Maine

Sharon D. Kruse
Professor and Assistant Chair, Department of Educational Foundations
  and Leadership
University of Akron
Akron, Ohio

Patricia Law
Principal, Granby Memorial High School
Granby, Connecticut

Sarah (Sally) Mackenzie
Associate Professor, Department of Educational Leadership
University of Maine
Orono, Maine

William A. Sommers
Director, Learning Alternatives Community School
Spring Lake Park, Minnesota

Visit **go.solution-tree.com/plcbooks** to download handouts and access materials related to this book.

# Table of Contents

■ ■ ■ ■ ■

# About the Author

■ ■ ■ ■ ■

 **Timothy D. Kanold, PhD,** is an award-winning educator, in-demand motivational speaker, and educational leader. He is former director of mathematics and science and served for five years as superintendent of Adlai E. Stevenson High School District 125, a model professional learning community district in Lincolnshire, Illinois. Dr. Kanold is founder and director of E²-PLC Learning Group, a professional development learning team committed to the pursuit of equity and excellence for students, faculty, and school administrators. He conducts professional development leadership seminars worldwide with a focus on systematic change initiatives that create and sustain greater equity, access, and success for all students.

He is a recent past president of the National Council of Supervisors of Mathematics (NCSM) and coauthor of several best-selling mathematics textbooks over two decades. He has served on writing and research commissions for the National Council of Teachers of Mathematics and was the lead writer and executive editor for the task-force development of *The PRIME Leadership Framework: Principles and Indicators for Mathematics Education Leaders* by NCSM. He has authored numerous articles and chapters on school leadership for education publications. Dr. Kanold received the prestigious international 2010 Damen Award for outstanding contributions to the field of education from Loyola University Chicago, the 1986 Presidential Award for Excellence in Mathematics and Science Teaching, the 1991 Outstanding Young Alumni Award (from Illinois State University), the 2001 Outstanding Alumni Award (from Addison Trail High School), and the 1994 Outstanding Administrator Award (from the Illinois State Board of Education). He received a bachelor's degree in education and a master's degree in mathematics from Illinois State University. He completed a master's in educational administration at the University of Illinois and earned a doctorate in educational leadership and philosophy from Loyola University Chicago.

To learn more about Dr. Kanold's work, visit his blog Turning Vision Into Action at tkanold.blogspot.com or follow tkanold or #plcleaders on Twitter.

To book Dr. Kanold for professional development, contact pd@solution-tree.com.

# Foreword

■ ■ ■ ■ ■

## Richard DuFour

We have all heard the story. The heroic leader arrives on the scene to overcome the collective deficiencies of the others in the organization through his or her extraordinary wisdom, courage, and charisma. We love this story, and we have repeated it in a variety of contexts—the lawman of the Old West who brings order out of chaos, the gifted athlete who single-handedly lifts the team to victory, the innovative CEO whose insights save the company, the passionate school principal who personally turns around a failing school, the military leader whose conviction and courage enable troops to vanquish the enemy despite overwhelming odds. In each, the gifted leader saves the less capable. We embrace poet Roger Robicheau's assertion that "the American Hero always comes through," because it is a story we have been told throughout our lives.

So if you are looking for another iteration of the mythic hero, *this book is not for you!* In *The Five Disciplines of PLC Leaders*, Tim Kanold offers a very different and far more accurate picture of contemporary leadership.

| The Great American Hero . . . | The PLC leader presented in *The Five Disciplines* . . . |
|---|---|
| • Is an extraordinary and rare individual, someone much different from the rest of us | • Recognizes that leadership can and should be widely dispersed and that people throughout the organization are capable of leading |
| • Is born, not made—someone destined to lead because of innate abilities and qualities | • Identifies specific skills essential to effective leadership, and purposefully trains to develop those skills |
| • Focuses on changing others | • Focuses first on changing himself or herself |
| • Not only has the answer to our problems, but is the answer to our problems | • Recognizes no one individual has all the answers, and focuses on asking the right questions for the collective consideration |

- Talks *to* others in the organization to ensure they are clear on the leader's expectations

- Is successful because he or she always *knows* what needs to be done

- Inspires others to follow him or her

- Leads us to success in the end

- Is irreplaceable

- Talks *with* others to create shared understanding and expectations

- Is successful because he or she is always *learning* what must be done, including the deep learning that comes from mistakes

- Inspires others to pursue shared vision and values

- Recognizes there is no end to implementing the PLC process

- Focuses on ensuring the continued success and ongoing improvement of the organization after he or she has left it

The stark contrast between the mythic leader and the leader of a professional learning community (PLC) that this book espouses is just one reason *The Five Disciplines* warrants the attention of educational leaders. Unlike many books that paint leadership with a broad brush—urging readers to create a shared vision, develop a results orientation, and become a servant leader—Kanold translates those desirable but vague concepts into specific steps that demand immediate action. He conveys a sense of urgency when he writes, "You cannot reach your full potential as a leader, or help others reach theirs, until you become intentional about imagining how the organization would look in three, five, or ten years, based on your actions *today*." Then, chapter after chapter, he goes beyond exhortation to offer explicit processes, detailed strategies, and compelling questions to help leaders move forward.

Throughout the book Kanold urges readers to reject what Collins and Porras (1997) have called the "tyranny of OR" and to instead embrace the "genius of AND." Leaders of professional learning communities must insist on adherence to vision and values *and* encourage individual autonomy and empowerment. They must focus on results *and* relationships. They must celebrate current efforts and achievements *and* be perpetually discontent with the status quo. They must hold others accountable *and* be accountable to others. They must have a positive influence on those who report to them *and* those to whom they report (as well as their peers). They must acknowledge their uncertainties and weaknesses *and* be absolutely certain of their ability to shape rather than merely experience the future. And very importantly, Kanold shows readers the steps they can take to bring the "genius of AND" to life in their schools.

Kanold draws upon educational researchers, organizational theorists, psychologists, students of leadership, and his own rich experience as a highly effective leader of a professional learning community to present a narrative that is personal, powerful, and tremendously persuasive. This is not a book to skim. It is a book that will require you to think, to reflect deeply on the questions that all PLC leaders must answer, to confront the brutal facts of your own leadership, and ultimately to develop new skills and knowledge vital to your success and the success of your school or district. It is a book that you will return to over and over again to explore its wisdom and advice.

In *Leaders of Learning: How District, School, and Classroom Leaders Improve Student Achievement*, Bob Marzano and I presented the premise that "every person who enters the field of education has both an opportunity and an obligation to be a leader." This book is a must-read for all educators who hope to fulfill that obligation.

# Professional Learning Community Leadership: Disciplined Leaders Required

*Few companies have a culture of discipline. When you have disciplined people, you don't need a hierarchy. When you have disciplined action, you don't need excessive controls. When you combine a culture of discipline with an ethic of entrepreneurship, you get the magical alchemy of great performance . . . disciplined leaders take disciplined action.*

—Jim Collins

*Humans, by their nature, seek purpose—a cause greater and more enduring than themselves.*

—Daniel Pink

Can you recall the specific moment when you became keenly aware that school leadership—at any level beyond the classroom and the student sphere—should become part of your personal purpose for your work life? Was it during a meaningful conversation (or several conversations over a period of time) with a colleague or friend? Was it inspired by an important relationship with a leadership mentor or trusted person? Was it a moment of self-discovery? You just *knew*. And the personal purpose for your work life collided with the crazy, fast-paced, and demanding world of district, school, or school program leadership.

For me, it was a sixth-period sophomore geometry class in the fall of 1984. I stood in front of the room at the chalkboard—whiteboards, computer-supported "smart" boards, and mobile content sharing were not yet on the scene. I used pale yellow chalk on a green board back then, and I was demonstrating a triangle congruence proof for my students. I had a moment of self-discovery that was crystal clear. As the "content teaching" words were coming out of my mouth, my brain was thinking: *I love my students, I love teaching, I love mathematics, I even love leading my students and coaching basketball. Teaching is my calling, I am sure of it. But I just need something more to challenge my professional life. I need to serve a broader purpose that will allow for an impact beyond the classroom walls.*

After twelve years as a full-time high school mathematics teacher (six years each in two school districts, interrupted by one year at a university) and additional prompting from influential leaders in my life, I began the journey that has now led to twenty-five years of adult leadership. Just like you, I intentionally chose the path of school leadership, not fully understanding the personal discipline, thinking, and continuous training it would require—especially as the professional learning community or PLC movement began to take hold.

I agreed to leave my current position as a full-time mathematics teacher and become the director of the Division of Mathematics and Science at a growing suburban Chicago high school district. Although the principal and the selection committee had chosen me for the position, the superintendent was not so sure. His endorsement at a social function at the beginning of the year might best be summarized as "He seems like a nice guy, but what does he really know about being a school *leader*?" At that moment, little could I realize that sixteen years later I would serve the district in his very capacity—as superintendent. My skill set at that time wasn't predictive of such a future, and the idea of becoming a superintendent someday just wasn't on my radar. I am sure it is the same for many of you reading these words. But you just never know where your leadership path will take you.

## The Paradoxes of Leadership

As I started my school leadership career, I was confident on the outside yet still learning about myself and about the leadership of others on the inside. In hindsight, I probably had just the right mix of doubt and the necessary confidence to lead well. I have talked to many school leaders who started out the same way, and they have been relieved to hear they weren't alone in the paradox of knowing just enough to understand that there was a lot they didn't know. This book, if anything, gives you—the school leader—permission to take focused risks, make mistakes, and most importantly, learn from those mistakes. Understanding that you don't fully know all the answers—and never will—is a paradox of leadership wisdom and an actual strength of PLC school leaders.

In *Hard Facts, Dangerous Half-Truths, and Total Nonsense* Jeffrey Pfeffer and Robert Sutton (2006) explain that leadership wisdom means

> striking a balance between arrogance (assuming you know more than you do) and insecurity (believing you know too little to act). This attitude enables people to act on their present knowledge while doubting what they know. It means they can do things now, as well as keep learning along the way. (p. 52)

In this book, we will examine how PLC school leaders learn to act at the right times and in the right way and with the right amount of energy, engagement, grace, and compassion. We will see how they practice particular *disciplines* to become comfortable with the many paradoxes of effective school leadership—among them, leading by serving, engaging through strategic disengagement, allowing autonomous behaviors within defined boundaries, and inspiring through humility.

For our purposes, we define a PLC leadership discipline as follows:

**A set of actions that you intentionally practice, through continuous training, to improve your ability to lead**

The five disciplines of PLC school leadership described in this book allow you to do what you cannot currently do by just *trying* harder. The disciplines focus your time, energy, and effort on personal skills that make you an outstanding professional learning community leader. As you continuously *train* to get better at each discipline, you will become more leadership "fit," and your discernment and wisdom will improve significantly over time.

# Training to Run the PLC Race

You can't just get up off the couch and *try* to run a marathon. If you tried hard, I suspect you could run some distance. You might make it three hundred yards. You might last two or three miles or maybe even ten miles. But without the proper training, you would not make it the full 26.2 miles, and you would suffer the physical and mental consequences of pushing yourself beyond your limits.

Similarly, running the race of successful school leadership is not about trying harder, especially if trying harder and working longer hours leave you feeling like you can barely keep up. (Chapter 4 will explain in detail how to master this "Red Queen" effect on your leadership energy.) The reality is that on most school days, the work of school leadership will exhaust you. You are trying hard to do your best, and you really can't try any harder.

But you *can* train harder. Some of the most common leadership questions are, Where do I focus my energy and effort as a PLC leader? How do I find the time to get it all done? How do I turn our vision into real action? How can I get better at PLC leadership? The theme of this book is that your true leadership work is to train in the disciplines that will enable you to lead well and that will transform *who you are* as a PLC school leader. This is where you should focus your leadership time, energy, and attention. Once you do that, the other questions will be answered. You will be able to lead your school far beyond superficial PLC performance, to exceptional PLC performance.

Trying hard to make good leadership decisions without the training necessary to identify the values and beliefs behind those decisions or to sustain the energy and engagement you need to be at your personal and professional best every day will eventually render you ineffective and frustrating to those closest to you—your family, your faculty, your students, your fellow administrators, and your friends. The high-energy demands and expectations of effective PLC leadership require you to lead a disciplined life. They require the pursuit of a better version of you—each day, each week, each month, each year—a version of you in which your current strengths have all become more highly developed through training *around the right set of disciplines.*

School leadership, as defined in this book, is not about job titles per se. All adults in the district or school lead and influence one way or another. In successful PLC schools, adults take ownership to act as positive leaders within their own personal sphere of influence, regardless of position or title. Think of every student and adult who has been influenced by your thoughts, words, actions, and inactions over the past five years. It starts to add up. You are leading and influencing others in the school community to go somewhere. The question is where?

The pursuit of the five disciplines is, of course, a conscious choice. You don't *have* to train yourself in them. Your leadership journey is personal, and filled with pain, disappointment, promise, and triumph. The PLC leader's life can be extremely rewarding, but it is really hard work. The results that accrue from becoming intentional about your leadership life can be humbling. If you do pursue the five disciplines, leadership will become much more than a job to you—you will be building a legacy—and in the end you will have tapped into your full leadership potential as well as the leadership potential of others.

# The Disciplined PLC Leader

How do you know if you are a well-disciplined PLC leader? A well-disciplined leader is someone who can discern when silence, healing words, low tolerance, empathy, grace, humor, gentleness, or tough love is needed. He or she assesses each situation promptly and responds with urgency, positive energy, and grace—day in, day out, month in, month out, year after year. The leader's actions and responses become what people really remember about the leader. (In other words, your actions determine what others say about you when you are not in the room or no longer at the school.)

What is disciplined action? As an effective PLC leader, you not only lead well, but you also reflect long enough to articulate to others, with great clarity, the values and beliefs that cause you to lead well. You know how you *think*. You can pinpoint the rationale for your actions and decision making with ease. Your reasoning is always connected to the simple and fundamental dual mission for schools: creating success for all students and ensuring individual and collective adult learning and growth. You understand that highly effective leadership is necessary to prevent school stagnation and a natural drift toward mediocre performance. Most importantly, you make decisions and act in ways consistent with the vision and values for your area of school leadership and routinely review the practices that you and your school are pursuing to determine if they are still aligned with the vision and values.

Finally, you base your daily leadership work on a series of *intentional* disciplines that transform your ability to lead a more authentic and deeply committed PLC culture. You come to work every day fully engaged, with positive energy. This everyday work eventually unfolds to become the story of your leadership life and the legacy you leave to the district, school, state, or province where you work.

# The Five Disciplines of School Leadership

To understand the choice of the five leadership disciplines described in this book requires an understanding of the context in which PLC school leadership resides. First, you must be crystal clear about what it means to effectively lead in a PLC school culture. What type of leadership is required for PLC growth and development? What type of leadership inhibits growth and development?

Second, you must be familiar with—and examine yourself for—the personal barriers that most often prevent PLC leaders from being able to lead with a high level of energy, positive judgment, discernment, and wisdom. That is, you must know yourself extremely well.

Third, you must identify specific personal leadership practices or experiences that will help you improve your discerning abilities and overcome the barriers to effective PLC development in your specific area of school leadership.

As stated earlier, the disciplines of a professional learning community leader are *intentional actions and practices* that enable him or her to become more effective. Qualities such as kindness, humility, or a positive attitude are valuable leadership traits, but they are not what this book means by disciplines. They are by-products of the disciplines. Should you decide to seriously pursue the PLC leader's life, you should commit yourself to continuous and lifelong improvement in five specific leadership disciplines:

1. Vision and values

2. Accountability and celebration

3. Service and sharing

4. Reflection and balance

5. Inspiration and influence

I do not pretend this is an exhaustive list of leadership disciplines. From my personal experience, however, I believe these five represent the most essential disciplines for improving your own performance and that of those within your professional learning community.

## The Discipline of Vision and Values

The discipline of vision and values is defined as follows:

> **The leadership work of developing and delivering a
> compelling picture of the school's future that produces
> energy, passion, and action in yourself and others**

As you grow in this discipline, you will develop a better understanding of your personal vision and values and how they connect to those of the school organization. You will be able to build a shared adult commitment to the vision and core values of a PLC for the school or district. You will ensure that the vision guides the decision-making actions for your district, school, or program area. You will learn to use vision and values as one of your most potent leadership tools for the development of coherent and sustainable actions.

## The Discipline of Accountability and Celebration

The discipline of accountability and celebration is defined as follows:

> **The leadership work of delivering specific improvement in student achievement results, and monitoring stakeholder actions that lead to those results, with consequences**

This discipline allows the professional learning community leader to overcome the barriers of stagnation, status-quo thinking, and fear of change. In other words, through accountability and celebration, you lead the transition from vision to realized action and implementation. As you grow in this discipline, you will learn to strike a balance between accountability and celebration, both of which are necessary to sustain continuous improvement.

## The Discipline of Service and Sharing

The discipline of service and sharing is defined as follows:

> **The leadership work of demonstrating personal accountability to the shared vision and to all who may be affected by your thoughts, words, actions, and inactions**

A PLC cannot fulfill its aim of building the knowledge capacity of all its members without building their *relational* capacity. The development of relational competence begins with the leader. As you grow in this discipline, you will shift your focus to serving the vision and serving the development of those in your sphere of influence. You will inspire others to broaden their focus in a similar way, creating an overall culture of service and sharing.

## The Discipline of Reflection and Balance

The discipline of reflection and balance is defined as follows:

> **The leadership work of intentionally and strategically engaging in and disengaging from high-energy activities**

As you grow in this discipline, you will come to understand the power of monitoring and managing the energy of your life. You will learn about the difference between time management and energy management. You will learn how to avoid an energy crisis and how to stay fully engaged in your daily leadership work. You will also learn how to help others become fully engaged in their work.

### The Discipline of Inspiration and Influence

The discipline of inspiration and influence is defined as follows:

> **The leadership work of consciously creating an enduring organizational legacy through the daily building of effective PLC practices and behaviors**

In the discipline of inspiration and influence, you become much more aware of the future impact of the actions you take today. You will develop a deeper understanding of practices that provide clarity and direction to the work of the organization. You will learn to *blaze the leadership path as you walk it.*

# The Benefits of Leadership Discipline Training

As a PLC leader, you must develop the confidence to believe you will be able to make great decisions on every issue, every day—decisions that stand up to the test of time—not because you try hard, but because you have trained hard to be able to do what is necessary when the moment arrives. Ultimately, when you become a *disciplined and well-trained* professional learning community leader, your judgment improves. Your wisdom level goes up. Your training and development eventually enable you to discern the right thing at the right time for the right reasons—most of the time. You are able to act with grace and positive purpose.

Sound Utopian? Perhaps, yet wise training on your part will help bring about a deep commitment to PLC tenets. The adults will be more fully engaged and alive in their work—they will become a highly motivated staff. However, know this—superficiality will always win the day if given the chance. All schools naturally drift toward easy, shallow PLC implementation unless a broad base of leaders—leaders like you—are pushing hard against the drift.

This is a *drift-resisting* leadership book. It explains how to do the daily "conditioning" necessary to move beyond superficiality into a leadership world filled with meaning, passion, purpose, action, and results. You may *know* what you need to do to train, but taking the initiative to step out the door and *do* the proper training will be a completely different challenge. Training in these five PLC leadership disciplines will be a lifelong pursuit—and if you don't train, you will not be in the leadership race for very long—at least not with much sense of satisfaction for you or your faculty, administration, and staff.

*The Five Disciplines of PLC Leadership* will force deep reflection. You may want to cycle through it many times. This book will be great for you if you like to journal. You may want to write in the book, use the study guides provided at the end of each chapter, pair up for a book study with someone you really trust, or complete a book study with your leadership team or collaborative learning team around one of the chapters.

I hope the five disciplines will resonate with your current leadership life, because if you are like me, you're trying really hard. Any truly meaningful human accomplishment requires perseverance. Your personal vision and values training will lead to greater *coherence* in your school organization work. Your personal accountability and celebration training will lead to a school organization that actually turns the vision into *realized action*. Your personal service and sharing leadership training will lead to *sustainable and more equitable* effort and action in your school organization. Your reflection and balance training will lead to a *fully energized, engaged, and committed* faculty and staff. And your inspiration and influence training will lead to a more *enjoyable, no-regrets* workplace—one that has your imprint, long after you are gone. At the end of your leadership race, you will have greater respect for the natural peaks and valleys of the leader's life. And you will be amazed at how your seasons of leadership training—year after school year—really mattered.

So let's get started. Let the training and the learning together begin.

# CHAPTER 1

## *The Discipline of*

# Vision and Values

■ ■ ■ ■ ■ *Every serious student of the subject asserts that leaders must have the capacity to envision an uplifting and ennobling image of the future and to enlist others in a common purpose. That's the good news. Here's the bad news. Today's leaders stink at it.*

—James Kouzes and Barry Posner

The concept of *vision* often feels vague and out of reach. Yet vision is and will be one of the most potent change weapons in your leadership life. Vision, when led extremely well, becomes the driver of change for your district, school, or program area. There are dozens of definitions of vision. My only caution is to be clear about the difference between *mission* and *vision*. Simply defined, mission is *why* your job and the school organization exist—your fundamental purpose. You can usually state the mission in one short sentence. For example, I subscribe to the PLC mission that is summed up in the simple mantra "Success for every student." Your mission—your reason for why the school or district exists—cannot be more complicated than for all adults to educate *as a PLC* in order to ensure the social, emotional, and academic success of every child.

On the other hand, vision moves the school organization beyond the question of *why* we exist to the question of *what* we should become. What are the most essential aspirations and pursuits that will guide current action, future direction, and your responsibility for improved results? Vision answers the question, are we really doing work that matters? Vision provides the focus and coherence necessary to avoid the natural drift toward mediocrity and stagnation. Vision describes how good we can become, and paints a picture of what it will look like when we get there.

For a leader, being able to rely on and teach about a rock-solid vision is essential. Indeed, it is the foundation of all other aspects of PLC leadership. With more than 1,300 leadership books on vision development alone, the case for the lifelong pursuit of improving your skill in this discipline is clear. Without a deep understanding of your personal vision and values, as well as the shared vision and values of the school organization, your leadership decision making will appear random, disjointed, and often disconnected. Those following you—those within your sphere of influence—will be left to wonder exactly where the school "ship" is headed.

Every school leader is capable of effectively developing a vision and teaching it well to others. You just have to train in the discipline. Let's review the definition of the discipline of vision and values:

**The leadership work of developing and delivering a compelling picture of the school's future that produces energy, passion, and action in yourself and others**

Effective PLC leaders are well trained in painting a compelling picture of a better future, enlisting others in its development, and using the vision to bring *sustained* coherence, clarity, energy, and focus to future adult commitments and actions for school or district programs. They embrace the word *imagine* to describe exciting possibilities of what could be:

- Imagine a school where every student has access to and equal opportunity for success in each grade level and each course within the curriculum.

- Imagine a school where every student has access to relevant, engaging, and meaningful learning experiences every day.

- Imagine a school where technology strategies are integrated into the student learning experience and used as a tool for engagement and motivation every day.

- Imagine a school where every faculty and staff member works interdependently and positively in a collaborative community to erase inequities in student learning.

- Imagine a school where every administrator, faculty member, and staff member is fully engaged in and enjoys his or her work.

- Imagine a school where every teacher uses formative and summative assessments that inform, enhance, and motivate student learning and improve instruction.

What is in your *imagine* list?

Your training in this discipline helps you to understand that a vision cannot be true or false but ultimately is evaluated against other possible directions for the school or district. A vision leader asks, Does our vision paint a picture that is better or worse than current practice? More or less appropriate? More or less compelling? More or less energizing? More or less ambitious?

A PLC leader must also be able to identify and articulate essential PLC *values*. You should be clear about the difference between *values* and *goals*. If mission addresses why we exist, and vision paints the picture of what we aspire to become someday, then values represent the *commitments to action* necessary to ensure the vision is realized. Goals represent the measurable student outcomes or results that will reveal whether the adult commitments to action and effort have actually helped move the organization or school program closer to the vision. Goals are the *outputs* of our work. Your adult work life is aimless unless it actually results in children who are both smart (able to demonstrate successful learning of essential knowledge and skills) and good (able to demonstrate good citizenship and positive moral character).

In a professional learning community, then, goals are distinct from values or commitments to action. And yet, mission, vision, values, and goals are woven tightly together. The PLC leader understands the vision will not be realized without adult commitment to the behaviors and actions that support it as well as evidence that the actions will lead to measurable improvement in student learning and development. In the best PLC cultures, vision and values ultimately become the driving force behind the decision-making process that takes place every day in a particular area of school leadership.

# Connecting Your Personal Vision and Values to Daily Decision Making

During my first year at Stevenson, as director of the Mathematics and Science Division (essentially a department chairmanship with assistant principal duties), I often struggled to make decisions that were best for my division and for the school. I simply had not yet developed the judgment required for good decision making. Teachers came to me with ideas, wanting my approval to move forward. I froze. Counselors called about a student placement decision. I froze. The school board wanted my written opinion on a new grading policy and its impact on future course enrollments. I froze. Some teachers wanted to integrate calculator use into our mathematics and science courses in grades 6–12, and others did not. They wanted to know where I stood and whom I would support. I froze. There were times when I actually made decisions and then got angry reactions from teachers and parents. I froze even more. And all along, I was *trying* really hard to be right, to be a strong leader.

In retrospect, I realize I had not yet done the training necessary to achieve personal vision and values clarity. I made decisions that I am sure were based on underlying beliefs; I just wasn't conscious of what those beliefs were or of how they related to my decisions. Although I was vaguely aware of my expectations for a vital, non-negotiable vision and the corresponding adult behaviors and values, I could not precisely list those expectations, nor could I clearly explain the beliefs behind them.

Not only was my discernment quotient pretty low, but so was the discernment quotient of those I was trying to lead and influence. We made lots of decisions, but if you asked any of us working within our emerging PLC *why* we were making those decisions, we could not easily explain ourselves. There was little coherence to our individual or collective decision making and actions. We rarely made decisions based on judgments designed to either advance or detract from a specific aspect of the vision; in fact, there was usually *no* basis for our decisions other than our opinions and instincts. And effective professional learning communities don't operate on a confidence level of instinct alone. Every decision must be tied to a well-researched conviction that it will advance the pursuit of the well-defined vision for the school or program.

The first step in your training to become a better vision leader, then, is to define your *personal vision* for your district, school, or program area. To teach and lead others well requires you to know your own vision and values, the beliefs underlying those values, and the sources that you rely on to give authority to your beliefs. Ask yourself, What future do I aspire to? What do I hope it will look like in action? Find pictures in your mind that represent the vision, and use those pictures to teach others about what could be.

For an exercise to learn more about your personal vision, visit **go.solution-tree .com/plcbooks** to download the worksheet *Decisions and Affirming Sources* (this site contains all the worksheets and tools to support this book). During the next two weeks, write down every decision you make at work—large or small. Next to each decision, write down the factors that informed it. *Your reasons for these decisions will reveal your beliefs as a leader.* What are your beliefs about what is truly best for student learning, instruction, and assessment? What do you believe about how best to develop adults' knowledge capacity and relational capacity? Do you believe there is a need for more grace in the workplace? Do you believe in equitable learning for every child? All of this will surface.

Well-disciplined vision leaders identify several reliable sources that can validate their beliefs. These sources provide checks and balances to determine whether you are pursuing the right things and building your personal vision on *actions* that will yield positive results. As you compile your two-week list of decisions and the reasons for those decisions, try to identify the various sources that informed and influenced your reasoning for each decision. Examples might be educational research; a mentor; a national-, provincial-, or state-level recommendation; a field-based observation; or a personal belief.

I discovered that my personal vision of what was best for all students in mathematics and science emerged from five reliable sources. Whenever I was having doubts as to whether I was supporting the right actions or practices, I would just check to see if these five sources also supported those actions and practices:

1. My own teaching experiences with what works and doesn't work for improved student achievement

2. My understanding of how research informs practice

3. The wisdom of my professional colleagues on the state and national levels

4. The wisdom of my two to three most trusted colleagues and mentors

5. The reality revealed by various data measures of student success

These reliable sources served as a great help to me over the years. I used this list as a way to seek input and advice before moving forward—especially if the decision was going to have a significant impact on the work behaviors of many adult stakeholders.

# Refining Your Personal Vision

Your personal vision—your compelling, energizing picture of the future—is an expression of the principles you are so passionate about that you will defend them, teach them, and lead others toward them. These principles allow you to lead with energy, consistency, and coherence. Take the time you need to be sure you know and understand them. Write them down. Memorize them. Live them, and be sure to publicly tie your daily decisions to them.

My personal vision for instructional leadership eventually distilled down to five main ideas. It took about four years before I was sure these images produced energy, passion, and action in me—and hopefully in those I was leading and influencing. Here is my vision list:

1. Every classroom will provide a relevant, meaningful, and connected curriculum with equitable levels of rigor every day.

2. Every classroom will create a learning experience that requires student engagement, communication with others, and active learning every day.

3. All end-of-unit assessments will reflect multiple levels of cognitive demand and be used formatively to improve teaching and learning.

4. Every student will experience technology as an aspect of teaching, learning, and assessment in every course or grade level.

5. Every grade-level and course teacher will actively participate in a collaborative, interdependent learning community for the purpose of improving student achievement.

This personal vision for instruction may or may not feel compelling to you, but it energized me. Eventually, these five "right things" became part of my everyday thinking and my teaching to those I was leading. They moved from vaguely hanging around in the back of my mind to having an impact on every moment and every decision I made. I trained to understand them better, know the research about them better (research trumps opinion), and communicate vivid pictures of their implementation better. I sought out every corner of our school and district where this vision wasn't happening and asked myself, what do I, as a leader, need to do better in order to close the gap between our aspirations and our current reality?

At some point in your leadership life, you, too, started to realize you had a personal vision for your program or area of school leadership. It might be why you accepted a specific leadership job. Is that vision crystal clear to you? The *Personal Vision Test* will help you to distill the main ideas of your vision (visit **go.solution-tree.com /plcbooks** to download the test). The test questions relate to the three to five right things for adult behaviors and commitments that you just know reflect your personal vision or aspiration for your area of leadership:

1. Are the items on my list crystal clear to me?

2. Can I speak to them with great clarity?

3. Can I easily identify them when they are in action and notice their absence when they are not in action?

4. Does my list fire me up? Does it create energy, passion, and purpose for me?

5. Why is each item on my list? What are the underlying beliefs that it reflects?

6. Do the items on my list appear to be in alignment with my core beliefs, or is there tension between the two?

7. How do I know this list is the right one for my school or area of leadership?

8. Does my list generate a compelling picture of the future?

9. Is my list based on reliable sources? What are they?

10. If I took my list and randomly surveyed various stakeholders—teachers, staff members, board members, other administrators, parents, and students—would their list of three to five right things match or align with mine?

A rock-solid school vision acts as a constraint on actions that are inconsistent with it. It is designed to unleash and then focus the energies of the school in a common direction for the greater good of student and adult learning. Although you need to understand your personal vision well, your ultimate goal is to merge the personal visions of all those in your sphere of influence into a single clear, concrete message about which adult actions will move your school closer to your desired future.

# Connecting Your Personal Passion to the Vision of Professional Learning Communities

Are you personally passionate about the vision of a PLC culture? Does the vision of professional learning communities match your values or actions and underlying beliefs? Do you have a clear understanding that the vision is first and foremost about adult and student behaviors and practices that will increase student learning? If not, you can try as hard as you want, but you will never be able to advance others toward the PLC vision. It is just too difficult, and it won't matter to you enough to fight the battle and do the hard work required to move others into a PLC culture. You will quickly be exhausted. To succeed, you must not only see the vision of professional learning communities with clarity; you must also *feel* so deeply about it that you will be able to inspire others to follow you in pursuing it.

Stevenson High School created a "Vision and Values" document that summarizes what it means to educate as a PLC (Adlai E. Stevenson High School, 2010). Here is an excerpt:

### Building a Professional Learning Community

In order to ensure "Success for Every Student," the Board of Education, administration, staff, students, parents, and community commit to collaborative practices that ensure continuous improvement and progress toward the vision. The collective expertise and passionate commitment to learning drives individuals to excellence in their fields. To attain this vision:

A. All members of the school community actively promote and uphold the District's mission, vision, values, and goals.

B. The District commits to recruiting, developing, and retaining individuals who embrace the school's mission, vision, values, and goals.

C. All adults commit to developing and contributing to high-performing collaborative teams to better serve and support all students.

D. All members of the learning community understand that personal and professional development depends on goal-setting resulting from thoughtful and critical reflection, which leads to continued learning and growth.

E. Everyone commits to innovation, collective inquiry, evidence-based decision-making, and reflects on the results of teaching and learning.

Can you envision a future in which all adults in your school improve practice by working together and learning from one another, build their knowledge capacity by looking at student work, and actively seek to improve the learning of all students—especially those most disadvantaged? Will this effort be carried out with a spirit of mutual support and trust? Now that is a vision to get fired up about!

When you lead the vision with passion, you energize others. It begins with you. You must own it. You must teach it. You must lead it. You must show others what it looks like. You must know when it is not in evidence. And you must use it to bring coherence and clarity to the work of the school. You must know and teach the collective vision so well that eventually it becomes the coherence provider for all of the "stuff" and daily decision making of the school or district. Consider what is happening in your area of school leadership. If the efforts of the faculty and staff lack coherence, then the problem is a weak organizational understanding of, and connection to, the vision. And if the vision is leaking, you need to look in one place: the mirror.

# Creating Vision Ownership for Sustainability

Although you must have a personal vision of the future, the vision of an uplifting and ennobling future never "sticks" in the school organization if the only person who owns that vision is the leader. All stakeholders must own the vision, and if they don't have a voice in its development, they will never completely honor it. Whatever your area of leadership influence, there must be a clearly defined process that solicits input from multiple voices to cast a well-informed vision that all will own and support. Trust and utilize the knowledge and skills of the various stakeholders (especially those most affected by the vision). This collaborative process of vision casting (or of revising a current vision) is as important as what the vision declares.

Creating a *shared vision* for each specific area of school leadership was a first order of business for all of the learning teams (faculty and administration) in our professional learning community at Stevenson. We used a vision casting process at every level of our school organization: district, school, and grade or course level. We wanted all departments and areas of the school program to develop rock-solid vision statements that would guide adult decision making and *be aligned* with the broader vision of the school district. Shared visions were created by all academic teaching and learning programs as well as the athletic program, counseling and student services, cocurricular activities, and the central office.

The vision casting process should always begin with the work of a task force or committee that represents stakeholders appropriate to that level: faculty, staff, board members, administrators, parents, or students. It is important to get input from all those affected by the vision before it is finalized. To frame and focus the discussions, ask the group to consider litmus-test questions such as these:

- Will the vision we create or revise be able to guide our future work and decision making by all stakeholders? If so, how?

- Will this vision inspire the involvement and participation of all stakeholders?

- Would you be excited to send your children to a school or a school program with this vision?

- Can you see where you will fit as a stakeholder in this vision? What changes in your behavior will be required once you commit to this vision?

- Will the new vision need to delete anything from the current vision (if there is one)?

- Are the components of this vision for our school or school program in alignment with the overall district vision?

- Can you imagine how this vision will help set priorities for action over the next several years? What will be some of those priorities?

(Visit **go.solution-tree.com/plcbooks** to download the worksheet *Analyzing the Vision Development Process*.)

Before the vision document can be presented to stakeholders for feedback, the task force needs to analyze the document's language and the process of developing it. This analysis can serve to increase the likelihood of obtaining broad and sustained ownership. You can focus this discussion on several critical questions:

- How will we prevent the perception that the vision has been forced on the community?

- How will we ensure that most parents, teachers, and students will be familiar with our vision?

- Does day-to-day adult and student behavior provide evidence we are moving toward the vision? What would our behavior look like if that were the case?

- Can members of the staff, faculty, and administration clearly articulate their own personal vision of an exemplary school or school program? Are there gaps between our developed vision and the personal visions of the faculty, staff, or administration?

- How can we help all members of the community believe in the vision and its message? Do we demonstrate what we value or do not value in our day-to-day actions? What can we do to better express our vision and values to others?

- Part of being a professional learning community is the emphasis on continuous growth, improvement, and change. How does our new vision demonstrate and reveal professional learning community priorities?

- What type of future lessons and stories from our community will we share that reflect action toward our vision?

Sharing the vision document drafts is an important step in engaging stakeholders in activities that eventually lead to changes in the status quo. Be aware that the language you use in vision casting and revision can influence stakeholders' perceptions of the process and their willingness to participate. Some school leaders talk about getting "buy-in," using statements such as "We need buy-in to this vision." Stakeholders may interpret "buy-in" as manipulation, whereas statements such as "We need to own this vision" may be more acceptable. Ownership signals real engagement and commitment to actions that reflect the vision.

## Teaching the Vision

The shared vision cast by the stakeholders and communicated by the leader speaks loudly. A simple yet compelling picture of the future, it enables all levels of stakeholders—teacher teams, school-site leadership teams, district and community teams—to say, "We know where we are headed, we know our aspirations, and we will not tolerate adult or student behaviors that act as barriers to the vision." In a professional learning community, declaring the vision is often an essential step toward creating expectations of certain vital behaviors. Once the vision is declared, you begin teaching for understanding of the vision and those expectations. Teaching the vision ensures coherent implementation by all adults in your leadership sphere of influence.

Leadership expert Noel Tichy (2002) states it like this: "Teaching is the most effective means through which a leader can lead . . . True learning takes place only when the leader/teacher invests the time and emotional energy to engage those around him or her in a dialogue that produces mutual understanding" (pp. 57–58). Tichy refers to the leader's "teachable point of view," or TPOV, which he defines as "a cohesive set of ideas and concepts that a person is able to clearly articulate to others" (2002, p. 74). You can apply the idea of a TPOV to any vision area of your school leadership life—for example, adult behaviors and practices related to student placement, formative and summative assessment, effective grading practices, school discipline, or the school's collaborative culture. Consider these questions as you examine adult behaviors and practices related to the vision:

- Who decides on changes to our behaviors and practices once the school year begins?

- How will these changes be communicated to affected stakeholders?

- Who has the final authority for instituting changes in our behaviors and practices?

- Have contributing factors regarding equitable opportunities for all students been critically examined?

- How can the decision leading to behavior and practice changes be evaluated for fairness and success?

- How will the vision components be used to resolve conflicts within our behaviors and practices?

Ultimately, you know your district or school TPOV works if faculty and staff *actually use it* to guide their daily thinking and decision making. The resulting coherence is one of the main reasons why the leadership discipline of vision and values is *the* place to start your PLC leadership journey. Skilled vision leaders teach the vision by posing the right questions, clearly articulating the vision, and helping those they lead connect every adult action and collaborative decision to the vision.

## Creating Vision Clarity

Dennis Sparks (2005) identified several fundamental barriers to professional learning communities, including "a lack of clarity regarding vision, values, intentions, and beliefs" (p. 162). A vision should provide a clear and coherent path for future actions. Whether the vision you are casting represents the school or the entire district, the goal is to help people to know, understand, and remember the main idea or the right things to become and to be about. Keep it very simple.

During a professional development session for about fifty team leaders in our school, we were engaged in our annual "vision-action" alignment check. In this activity, our leadership team examined the current and planned actions for each area of the school to identify any gaps between those actions and the overall district vision. One of our social studies team leaders suggested, "Why don't we just call our five main ideas the 'Five Es'?"

It took some creative rewriting, of course, to turn each element of our vision into a word that begins with *e*. Here is the section of Stevenson's "Vision and Values" document (Kanold, 2006) that spells out the Five Es:

1. ***Excellence* in curriculum, instruction, and assessment.**
   We will ensure the curriculum, instruction, and assessments represent the best practices in our profession. While accommodating individual student differences, interests, and abilities, excellence demands we develop a common, coherent, rigorous curriculum that actively engages all students.

2. ***Equity* and access for all students.**
   We will challenge each student to give his or her best effort intellectually and ethically. Adults must exhibit genuine care and concern for each student and must collectively commit to providing opportunities for students to fully access the curriculum at its most rigorous levels.

3. ***Educating* as a professional learning community.**
   We will commit to ongoing professional development as a model of life-long learning. The board, administration, and faculty must function in high-performing, collaborative teams focused on student achievement. Staff development is a job-embedded and collaborative process, not a singular event.

4. ***Environment* for learning.**
   We must provide an emotionally and physically safe, supportive learning environment. In this collaborative culture, we treat our diverse community of students and staff with respect, consideration, and acceptance, recognizing that learning is a dynamic and socially constructed process requiring engagement and supportive relationships with one's peers and teachers.

5. ***Engagement* with the community.**
   We will value the importance of collaborative relationships with our extended community—families, residents, businesses, government agencies, and education systems. We must strive to serve as a lighthouse, interacting and collaborating with the educational community. (p. 18)

The Five Es provided an image of what we were trying to become and gave us insight into our collective responsibilities and obligations for all future behaviors and practices. They became a staple part of our vision communication to all PLC stakeholders. Each week, I would either call or run into random faculty or staff members and ask them to state one of the Five Es they could remember. What did they think it meant? How did it affect them in their work? Were we in pursuit of the better future described in the E? If they could not remember one of the Es, I would give them a wallet card with the Five Es printed on it. Although the vision itself had much deeper meaning in its application, the Five Es helped us "mind the gap" between these five essential vision elements and the corresponding values or actions.

Mnemonic devices like the Five Es keep the vision simple and easy to remember, identify, and own. They make the beliefs behind the vision crystal clear. More importantly, once the vision is public, then expectations (of the vision) have been declared, and the "vision gap" is revealed. As the leader, are you prepared to monitor this gap and teach others how to close it? Do you know the level of implementation or lack of implementation you are willing to tolerate?

Vision casting is about much more than saying, "Let's seek this better future." Public vision casting directs the monitoring and accountability energy for the daily work of the school and focuses adult behavior for the next three to five years. It nurtures and insists on sustained adult action toward the vision.

# Creating Vision Alignment and Focus

By 1993, despite a major revision of our shared district vision document in 1990, the vision was not, in my opinion, being lived throughout our professional learning community of mathematics and science. I understood that while leaders should involve others in shaping the vision and direction of adult work and effort, ultimately it was my responsibility, as well as that of others on our leadership team, to ensure a responsive action to our vision among the seventy adults within my direct leadership influence. Yet seven years into my leadership journey, only a handful of faculty and staff demonstrated daily commitment to a fully engaged focus on our vision for teaching and learning mathematics. I had little practice at how to ensure the next step of vision leadership: alignment and focus.

For the past three years, we had been working diligently on explicating three of the five Es: *excellence* in curriculum, instruction, and assessment; *equity* and access for all students; and *educating* as a professional learning community. We had created ten specific faculty and staff actions within our area of the school program to achieve the three Es. Our efforts produced these ten adult-action statements:

### *Excellence* in Curriculum, Instruction, and Assessment
1.  The curriculum will reflect research-affirmed best practice and strategic use of technology.

2. Assessment will be an ongoing practice containing both formative and summative components for students and teachers.

3. Assessment will be used to ensure quality learning and to inform teachers and teams regarding curricular and instructional decision-making.

4. Curriculum, instruction, and assessment will reflect the District's support of innovation and commitment to continuous improvement in classroom instruction.

**_Equity_ and Access for All Students**

5. Students will fulfill the expectations that they will be actively engaged and give their best efforts, intellectually and ethically.

6. Attention will be paid to the whole student's emotional well-being and guide students in accepting increasing responsibility for their learning decisions and actions.

7. Every teacher will address gaps in achievement expectations for all student populations.

**_Educating_ as a Professional Learning Community**

8. We will commit to contributing to high-performing, collaborative teams.

9. We will commit to collective inquiry and reflection on the results of student achievement in order to improve student learning.

10. We will commit to a high level of mutual support and trust between all members of the learning community.

Our adult work and effort were aligned to the Five Es—or so I thought. My observations of our teacher learning teams in mathematics and science, our division office staff, our counseling department, our communication with parents, and our actions, however, indicated otherwise. There was a clear disconnect between our daily work and the ten vision actions. We were out of alignment with the vision and with each other, despite the creation of what I thought was a clearly articulated vision with yearly "team level" goals and plans for action. They were just that— plans. The plans were not being fully implemented.

In monitoring our activity, I recognized overwhelming evidence that we had lost our central focus. Many of our assessments were _not_ of high quality. Many teachers were _not_ working effectively in teams to develop and build formative assessments (even though we _said_ we were doing so). Many students were neither engaged nor required to engage in meaningful classroom dialogue. And there was evidence that our counselors and teachers—without a plan to stop the flow—still funneled certain types of students into lower-level courses. What had happened?

As the vision leader, I had made three fatal mistakes.

1. I had failed to clearly communicate how the vision might "look" in action. My teachable point of view was weak in terms of modeling and teaching best practice actions and solutions to others.

2. I had failed to understand it was my job to be the primary steward, teacher, and champion of the vision once it was declared—and I was slow to recognize when the vision was absent in the reality of our practice.

3. I thought those I led would serve the vision *because I said they should.* I had failed to *plan* practices to sustain the vision—such as nurturing other champions to speak for the vision or consistently referring to the vision as a voice of authority behind my decisions.

Ultimately, we simply had too many "main thing" actions on our plate. For those three E-vision components alone, we had ten areas of focused action. No wonder we were all exhausted and dispersed in our focus! I knew we couldn't operate as if everyone was the ruler of his or her own kingdom, his or her own source of authority. Chaos would reign. Actually, chaos *was* reigning. Coherence was losing the day, and the only thing we were sustaining was our individual ability to do our own thing. More importantly, student learning was not improving at rates we all thought were possible.

I was almost panicked that our central purpose was getting lost: *success for every student in mathematics and science.* So, what should a PLC leader do? I assembled a small team of influential stakeholders and thought leaders in mathematics and science (eight teachers, one counselor, and one English as a second language specialist). We worked together for three months to create a narrower and more appropriate focus for our area of the school. Specifically, we stated:

> An exemplary mathematics and science program articulates the outcomes it seeks for all of its students and monitors and assesses each student's attainment of those outcomes daily. We will ensure:
>
> 1. The curriculum addresses important, relevant, and meaningful academic content every day.
>
> 2. Assessment strategies reflect high-quality summative exams and formative assessment loops.
>
> 3. Instructional strategies reflect best practice and stimulate student engagement every day.
>
> 4. Instructional practice promotes and integrates technology to enhance curricular outcomes.

We reduced the focus of our exemplary work actions and effort down from ten to four "main thing" vision actions. The committee shared this list with all of the faculty and staff stakeholders in our area of school leadership for input and advice. In an effort to provide faculty learning teams with a foundation for informed decision making in the future, the task force provided needed professional development for these four vital vision elements and allowed a final opportunity for professional input. I personally led heartfelt and difficult discussions about the need for every adult in the room to honor these four elements of our vision. Though my leadership voice certainly had an influence on our future direction, the vision found its real authority through the work of multiple faculty and staff stakeholders. By limiting the breadth of our focus, we increased our chances of authentic implementation.

The only question still lingering was whether our professional learning community felt any professional obligation to follow this more focused vision and set of actions. So we recast the vision actions using "we will" commitment statements and aligned these commitment statements to recommendations from reliable and extrinsic sources: research, national professional organizations, and experts in the field. Finally, we connected our vision actions to potential and expected achievement results for improvement.

Once established, *the vision becomes the voice of authority for our work and actions.* A leader in a professional learning community is committed to this adage: "A shared followership is built not on *who* to follow, but on *what* to follow." The voice of the vision and values, not the voice of a single person, must win the day in a professional learning community. The work of the PLC leader is to know the shared vision, defend it, teach it, and inspire others to share and own it. Your leadership must spotlight all actions or inactions as either supportive or not supportive of advancement toward fulfilling the shared vision. According to James MacGregor Burns (1978), this type of vision adherence is part of a transformational leadership process in which leaders and followers help each other to advance to a higher level of purpose and motivation.

You cannot move away from the temporary extrinsic motivators of your personal leadership authority (you are the boss) until you have a shared vision that is owned by those you lead. Once the shared vision exists, you then become the lead teacher and steward of the more sustainable and intrinsic voice of authority (the vision is the boss) that emerges from the expectations of the shared vision. PLC school leaders face the delicate task of championing action mandates for the current vision while simultaneously engaging stakeholders in the effort to revise, focus, and improve that vision.

# Improving Vision Through Double-Loop Learning

In his book *Images of Organization*, Gareth Morgan (1997) asks, "Can organizations *learn to learn?*" (p. 84, emphasis added). To describe organizational learning, Morgan contrasts what he calls single-loop learning with double-loop learning. Single-loop learning has just three steps. In Step 1, you assess the current reality as evidenced in actions and results: what are we actually doing? In Step 2, you compare the current reality against the vision expectations: what are the right things we've committed to do? In Step 3, you take action on your analysis, making corrections as needed for any discrepancies between the reality of "the way we do things around here" and the vision pursuit of the *right* way to do things around here.

However, from time to time, every healthy school organization at all levels—district, school, program area, grade, and course—pauses the action cycle to ask, are the right things defined in the vision still appropriate? For example, you might ask, is our vision for student-engaged learning still a worthy pursuit? The answer might be yes, or the answer might be yes with some adjustments. Morgan (1997) describes this re-evaluation as *double-loop learning* and the step of examining the vision as *Step 2a thinking*: a process of "questioning whether or not the operating norms or vision elements are still appropriate" (p. 87). Figure 1.1 describes the concepts of single-loop and double-loop learning.

Can your learning team, school, or district learn to learn? The introduction of Step 2a in the process of recasting the vision is critical to the success of an organization to learn. Without Step 2a, "groupthink" can result in the failure of the organization to learn and grow from its own experiences and to adjust the vision for a new day. The prevailing mantra becomes "If it ain't broke, don't fix it" or "That is just the way we do things around here," and the status quo will prevail— even in a PLC culture. Just because the vision was cast at one point in time does not mean it is still the best vision for 2015, 2018, or beyond. In reality, this vision and values review ensures the school organization remains open to new ideas and evolving best-practice thinking. As a leader, does your vision casting process require the faculty and staff to practice Step 2a thinking?

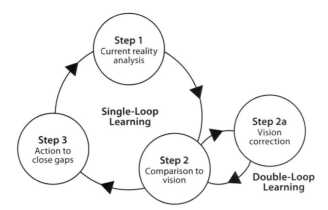

Step 1. Facts on current reality and behaviors are gathered.

Step 2. Current reality is compared to the vision of the right things of the PLC work.

Step 2a. Periodically, vision is checked: does it still define the right things we are to pursue?

Step 3. Corrections to reality are made to close the vision or revised vision gap.

**Figure 1.1: Double-loop learning and Step 2a thinking.**

*Source: G. Morgan (1997),* Images of Organization (2nd ed.), *Thousand Oaks, CA: Sage, p. 87. Used with permission.*

*Visit **go.solution-tree.com/plcbooks** to download a reproducible version of this figure.*

In a sense, Step 2a provides a built-in formative assessment process for vision-action growth and improvement. The work of teams of educators is cyclical. There is a start and end to every school year as well as every unit of instruction. Your leadership responsibility is to ensure the various PLC teams under your influence formatively examine all curricular, instructional, and assessment tasks on an ongoing basis—this might be weekly, monthly, or yearly. Every action by the team is up for 2a thinking and consideration during each period of reflection. The team always seeks to ask, Is there a better way we could work on this task? Are there better results we could achieve?

Your district, school, or program will benefit from this cathartic process of "creating anew" ownership in your key values, and leaders who inspire an "ever-learning" attitude in their professional learning communities will see them flourish and thrive.

## 25.1 and Beyond

We knew our school needed to become markedly different if we were to seriously pursue successful college preparatory performance for *all* our students—including those in the bottom 50 percent of their class, those on individualized education programs (IEPs), those in English learner (EL) classes, or others severely unprepared for the academic rigors and expectations of college. We were going to have to leave the harbor of limitations for the open sea of no limitations. There would be no more quotas for access into accelerated and honors classes. There would be no more caps on expectations for performance, preparation, access, or opportunity to the core curriculum and beyond.

For our college-bound high school students in the bottom half of their class, the American College Test or ACT (administered in the spring of their junior year) was the primary high-stakes exam for college acceptance in the Midwest. A good score was essential to college entrance. During the 1980s, our student ACT performance seemed subject to an artificial ceiling of a 22.0 composite (the national composite at the time was 20.7). Our students just couldn't seem to break through that barrier despite our best efforts. Several of our adults indicated this was the "best our students could do." Some of our faculty and administrators could not envision a senior class of a thousand students with an average ACT score of 25. It would never happen, they said.

But not all the faculty and staff felt or thought that way. They wanted to teach our junior students. They wanted to help students in the bottom half of their class have a chance to go to college. Then in 1990, the students broke through the 23 barrier and headed for 24, with the help of our focused faculty and staff. Six years later, in 1996, they broke the 24 barrier with a composite score of 24.2. And then our school leadership and several faculty said, "Why not try for 25? That would be exceptional greatness." For a long time 25.0 was a stretch goal that just could not be achieved. Yet the students slowly climbed toward the target of 25.0, an achievement that was only a dream twenty years previous. The 25.1 composite score achieved by the class of 2005 was another ceiling breaker, showing the unlimited potential and possibility of our students and our adults. In 1985 these results were thought to be impossible to reach, and our K–12 community had to respond despite the lack of belief. Your school too—your adults and students—can choose to pursue excellence far beyond current beliefs and understanding. Your vision is what you aspire to become and achieve.

It took ten years, and there was a big school celebration. Most assuredly, the celebration was not for the number 25.1. The celebration was for our journey and for our belief in the possibility of no limitations. The celebration was for the daily effort of hundreds of adults who maintained our heading toward the "true north" destination of our vision. We distributed small compasses that day. Every adult received the compass as a symbol for his or her role in opening the doors of possibility for our students. The back of the compass read, "Heading true north."

The day we celebrated the 25.1 achievement, I stated:

> *Regardless of your role in our school—from operations and support, to classroom teaching and learning—you have helped to create a culture of expected excellence, equity, safety, understanding, engagement, and community. All, not just a few, have nurtured our learning community culture. These results are due to so many who refuse to say no to the passion of possibility and who have embedded the vision of our school into their daily lives and into the way they work together.*

Of course, I did what every good PLC leader would do once a goal is achieved. I said, "Let's go for 26!" I am sure some thought that was another ceiling we could never break through. I personally imagined it would probably take another ten years, if not more.

And then in 2010 it happened. The 1,062 students in the class of 2010, with the support and encouragement of the administration, faculty, and staff, achieved an ACT composite score of 26.2. Who could have imagined it? Who was willing to imagine it? Once again what was an outrageous goal became reality. 27.0, anyone?

Søren Kierkegaard is quoted as saying:

> If I were to wish for anything I should not wish for wealth and power, but for the passionate sense of what can be, for the eye, which, ever young and ardent, sees the possible. Pleasure disappoints, possibility never. And what wine is so sparkling, what so fragrant, what as intoxicating as possibility? (GoodReads, 2010)

What is next for you and your district, school, or program? What barrier will you and your staff shatter in the next five years? In the next ten years? Can you name it? Is there a goal so lofty even your most ardent leaders can doubt it *and* get excited about it? I don't know what target beckons to you, but I do know you will break through seemingly impossible barriers. You will cast a "knock their socks off" vision, and with the right leadership, you will surprise even yourself. It is what effective PLC cultures *do*—they accomplish great things, one step at a time.

You wouldn't be reading this book if you weren't training to get better at that "vision thing." I know this. *Your* school, *your* district, and *your* area of leadership will not get better without great clarity on a shared vision of what that better day will look like—*so paint that picture, and let everyone have a chance to touch the brush.*

# Study Guide ▪ ▪ ▪ ▪ ▪

Visit **go.solution-tree.com/plcbooks** to download this study guide and the worksheets mentioned in it.

## *Examining My Leadership Perspective*

1. What do you remember about your decision to become a school leader? Did it surprise you? Why did you make that decision?

2. What is your vision for your area of school leadership? Is it widely shared and accepted? How do you know?

3. How do you and those on your leadership team or teacher team intentionally deliver a compelling picture of the future that produces energy and passion in others? What information will you use to justify the decisions you are making? Download the worksheet *Decisions and Affirming Sources*, and complete the activity.

4. Vision describes boundaries for action, boundaries that provide coherence to the efforts of the adults within the school and the learning community. In what way(s) have you or those you lead experienced vision-imposed boundaries recently?

5. What was the most meaningful aspect of this chapter for you? How will you use this material to apply the discipline of vision and values in your leadership role?

## *Extending My Leadership Perspective*

1. Think about your daily messages as a school leader. Do they reflect the values of the school or district? How do you know? What about the daily words and messages of your leadership or teacher team?

2. Page 26 describes three fatal leadership mistakes that can impede the sustainability of the vision. What fatal mistakes have you observed in your own leadership activities? In the activities of others on your leadership or teacher team?

3. Create a historical "PLC Vision Implementation" timeline for your district, school, or area of school leadership. Mark ticks on a horizontal line to indicate significant events in your history of becoming a professional learning community; between the marks, note the vision lessons learned along the way.

4. Stevenson's Five Es (page 23) describe five general vision themes: excellence, equity, educating as a PLC, environment, and engagement with

the community. Describe a simple yet clear method to communicate your overall vision themes for your district, school, or area of school leadership.

5. Download the *Personal Vision Test*. What do your answers to this test reveal about your vision actions? Are too many "main thing" vision actions expected this year? If so, as a leader, what priorities will you set? How do you plan to communicate these priorities to others?

6. What process are you using to develop the vision? To guide the team's discussion of the process, refer to the worksheet *Analyzing the Vision Development Process*.

7. Prepare your one-minute professional learning community teachable point of view (TPOV) for your area of school leadership. Who will you invite to critique your TPOV?

8. A disciplined vision leader intentionally pursues double-loop learning (see fig. 1.1, page 29). Identify the specific area of your school leadership that could use the adjustments and corrective process of Step 2a thinking. How could you build Step 2a thinking into the normal rhythm and cycle of the school year? Download and share the figure *Double Loop-Learning and Step 2a Thinking*.

9. What is your "25.1" pursuit? Describe the no-limitations student achievement story you hope to tell someday.

CHAPTER 2

*The Discipline of*

# Accountability
# and Celebration

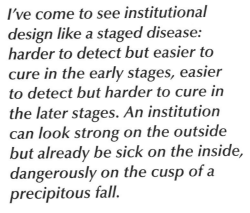

*I've come to see institutional design like a staged disease: harder to detect but easier to cure in the early stages, easier to detect but harder to cure in the later stages. An institution can look strong on the outside but already be sick on the inside, dangerously on the cusp of a precipitous fall.*

—Jim Collins

As of this book's writing, there were 53,963 books on leaders and 3,087 books on school leaders at Amazon.com. Writing about the unique aspects of school leadership—especially the leadership of a shared vision by all stakeholders—has significantly fewer voices in the educational community. On the subject of vision leadership, there were 1,398 books on vision development and 131 books on vision implementation. There is a reason there are ten times as many books on vision creation and development as there are on vision action and implementation. It is just so hard to turn vision into realized action.

Through the leadership discipline of accountability and celebration, it is possible to create a culture in which all adults engage in the difficult work of turning the school's vision into implemented action. And to master this discipline requires deep management and leadership skills in harmony with one another. This discipline requires effective monitoring of action—management.  It also requires brokering of action, change, and shifts to meet the vision—leadership. You must manage and lead others toward the vision.

How do you gain confidence that you can manage *and* lead the transfer of vision into practice? To paraphrase John Kotter (1999), strong school leadership with no management risks chaos. Strong management without leadership entrenches the school or district into a deadly bureaucracy with little engagement and almost no accountability for implementation. Do we really have to collaborate and *do* any of this vision stuff? is the silent, or sometimes not too silent, question asked by many of the adults in our sphere of leadership influence.

Although good management skills are necessary to support vision implementation and action, they are not sufficient. Through good management you can create a great vision for your area of school leadership and support structures for that vision. Yet it takes leadership skill to transition those you lead into actual implementation of and action on the vision. Leadership creates the relationships and designs the strategies of accountability and celebration necessary to make the vision come alive.

Your ability to turn vision into action is built upon the foundation and trained practice in the discipline of *accountability and celebration*. Let's review the definition of this discipline:

> **The leadership work of delivering specific improvement in
> student achievement results and monitoring stakeholder
> actions that lead to those results, with consequences**

These two elements of this discipline of school leadership, accountability and celebration, are tightly interwoven. Both are necessary to drive every continuous improvement effort you will lead. Accountability without celebration—of improved results and the adult actions that led to those results—leads to diminished hope, uncertainty, disengagement, and a general lack of awareness that action and implementation of the vision actually make a difference. Celebration without accountability leads to superficial festivity that is emotionally empty at best and promotes a random or false sense of progress at worst.

Thus, this leadership discipline presents these practices as an intricately matched, interdependent pair. Together they define the fundamental leadership practices that turn vision into action, implementation, and reality.

Accountability and celebration are the leadership glue for sustainable continuous improvement and growth toward the vision, and yet they are extremely difficult to do well. Lack of clear definition and purpose has rendered *accountability* and *celebration* as often misunderstood and negative terms. Even if we understand them as essential leadership practices, we often fail to implement them well. Thinking about the attributes of the terms *accountability* and *celebration* provides insight into how individuals may respond to them. The matrix in table 2.1 provides examples of the attributes of each term. (Visit **go.solution-tree.com /plcbooks** to download a reproducible version of this matrix on which you can list your own attributes of each term.)

Table 2.1 Accountability-Celebration Matrix

| Accountability | Celebration |
|---|---|
| Punishing | Positive |
| Failure | Energizing |
| Pressure | Encouraging |
| Negative | Joy |
| Stress | Progress |
| Blame | Hope |
| Unfair expectations | Hard to do well |
| Something done to me | Something I do for others |

Under *Accountability* (table 2.1), leaders often list words like *punishing, failure, negative efforts, stress, pressure, blame, unfair standards, unfair expectations, quality assurance, district or state reports,* and *mandates.* Often referenced as the *hand* of leadership, accountability represents a limited (although essential) lens on your role as a leader (Sergiovanni, 2005). The very word places most school leaders on the defensive. To many, accountability seems like something done to you by someone else. One definition rendered by the Education Commission of the

States (2010, p. 1) indicated that "accountability means holding key individuals and groups responsible for student achievement." The thought that others are holding you accountable feels aggravating. What right do they have to do so? And who exactly are *they*, anyway?

Can accountability really become a positive feature in your school culture? Or are school leaders—even those in a professional learning community—destined to accept the negative consequences and feelings caused by this word and action? As a skilled PLC leader willing to do the hard work of training in the discipline of accountability and celebration, this is a battle you *can* win. Accountability can become a vibrant and positive, almost invisible aspect of your school culture, but it will require a well-managed and well-led accountability and celebration system for continuous improvement for the adults and the students—a system that is also led by the leader's heart. Your passion for the vision will be demonstrated by how you address issues related to accountability and celebration.

Now take a look at the words under the *Celebration* column in table 2.1 (page 37). Words such as *happy, positive, energizing, gratitude, joy, fun, progress, hope,* and *noticed effort* surface. Phrases such as *not enough time, hard to do well,* or *someone's feelings will be hurt* might also emerge. Celebrations often seem more like something you do (or fail to do) for someone else. Referenced as the *heart* of leadership by Thomas Sergiovanni (2005), celebrations reveal your personal beliefs, values, and hopes for the school organization.

Well-led celebrations, moments that are used to extol or praise others, also serve the dual purpose of accountability. Leaders well trained in the discipline of accountability and celebration embrace celebrating student achievement results *and* adult actions that are consistent with and advance the vision and values of the district, school, or school program.

The well-disciplined professional learning community leader realizes there are two primary types of accountability and celebration targets in a professional learning community:

1. Accountability for and celebration of improved student results

2. Accountability for and celebration of stakeholder actions toward the shared vision of the school

Most professional learning community leaders understand the idea of student achievement goals and the accountability to and celebration of results. It is the second type of accountability and celebration that is often most confused, diffused, and ignored: *accountability to action*.

The definition of this leadership discipline requires PLC leaders to promise both accountability and celebration to those they lead. Your real leadership work in creating an effective system of accountability and celebration begins with your response to the monitoring of results and adult actions combined with your understanding of the "with consequences" aspect of this leadership discipline.

# The Courage to Do More Than Monitor

Why is it so hard for PLC leaders to become comfortable monitoring progress on expected vision actions to the degree that is necessary for success? One of the most essential leadership questions you can ask yourself for turning vision into action is *How do I feel, on a deep-down gut level, about the school or program vision components?* Are you willing to take the time necessary to actively monitor adult behavior for the implementation of the declared vision and its related actions? If your monitoring reveals that something is not being implemented, does that bother you enough to want to do something about it?

It is at this moment that management indifference ends (you did monitor what was going on, after all) and true leadership begins (you refuse to accept that the vision is not being realized). Management requires the courage to *monitor*; it does not necessarily require you to do anything about what you observed—or to realize that it will take all of your skill to bring those you are leading back onto the path toward the vision. Leadership requires you to *respond* to what you learn during the monitoring process. Daniel Goleman (as quoted in Schwartz, 2010, p. 24) states it like this:

> The range of what we think and do
>
> Is limited by what we fail to notice
>
> And because we fail to notice
>
> That we fail to notice
>
> There is little we can do
>
> To change
>
> Until we notice
>
> How failing to notice
>
> Shapes our thoughts and deeds.

What you choose to do with the results of your monitoring or *noticing*, and how you choose to use the information to influence the behavior of others, is the measure of your leadership and your discipline regarding celebration and accountability *for improved results, with consequences*.

The courage to lead is forged when something personally meaningful is at stake for you and for those in your sphere of influence. The vision must really matter to you. For example, consider the vision of instruction that *actively* engages all students every day. What happens as you monitor the teaching and learning methods of instruction that take place in the classrooms for your area of school leadership? Based on what you observe you must decide, Do I speak, or do I stay silent? Do I take action, or do I allow inaction? Courageous leadership action comes from your commitment to your deeply held beliefs about the issue—in this case, student-engaged learning. You can't have one without the other. Failing to notice might shape your thoughts and deeds, as Goleman says, but failing to do anything with what you notice is even worse.

As a professional learning community leader, you cannot respond to and close the vision gap if you don't *monitor* and inspect the reality of current actions by all stakeholders—parents, students, faculty, staff, and colleagues. But monitoring and noticing what is going on is of no value if the leader fails to act on the data collected. The PLC leader well trained in accountability and celebration understands that *responding* to data is critical to sustainability. Perhaps the new modern-day mantra should be "What gets held up for accountability and celebration is what gets done." The pressure—in a professional learning community—is on the vision. What really matters is the vision for an accountability and celebration response and how the leader delivers that response.

A PLC culture of accountability and celebration is only successful, however, when leaders monitor for the right set of adult behaviors.

# Monitoring the "Right Things"

A disciplined PLC vision implementation leader will use a set of criteria based on reliable sources to judge the pursuit of right things. For example, a PLC leader will ask, how do we know if instruction that "actively engages all students" is a right-thing behavior for all adults to pursue? Your leadership must provide a set of criteria upon which you and others can make that judgment with a high degree of certainty. These criteria should be based on reliable sources you have used to inform your own behavior. Criteria for student-engaged learning might include, for example:

- Is student engagement a vital aspect of lesson planning for you? Does lack of student engagement raise your ire?

- Is there research that supports and connects this vital adult and student behavior to improved student achievement? [For research on student engagement, see Marzano, 2007, and Marzano & Pickering, 2011.]

- Is there local district or school-site data evidence from classroom teachers who employ this vision for student learning? Do they experience higher rates of student success than those who don't employ this vision? How will you share this information with others?

- Are there recommendations from national commissions and research organizations that support this vision action as a "right thing" connected to improved student achievement?

You can use sample criteria such as these to check in on any "right thing" behavior. If the answers to these kinds of questions from reliable sources of information are yes, and the vision of the school or district demands it, then the behavior becomes a non-negotiable action and expectation for all adults. Either you lead the faculty, staff, and other stakeholders as needed toward the implementation of it, or you don't. Either you close the gap for your hopes or aspirations for the vision, or you don't. Either you respond to those not engaged in the vision, or you don't. You monitor vital adult actions and behaviors, you monitor results, and then it is time to act. It is time to lead and restore others toward the right things. It is time to celebrate those engaged in the right things. What will you do to turn vision into reality?

# Getting to "Loose-Tight" Leadership

The term *loose-tight* implies a combination of central leadership direction (tight) and participative decision making and individual freedom to make decisions (loose). These seemingly opposite demands of the practices of either tight, demanding leadership (do as I say—top-down decision making) or loose, participative leadership (do what you want—bottom-up decision making) were brought together in the 1982 book *In Search of Excellence* by Tom Peters and Robert Waterman. The term *loose-tight leadership* posed these paradoxical ideas not as an "or" proposition, but rather as an "and" statement. Is it possible that a school leader could be "tight"—that is, direct the decision-making process—*and* be "loose"—that is, allow for participative decision making—at the same time?

By 2002, Sagie, Zaidman, Amichai-Hamburger, Te'eni, and Schwartz demonstrated the positive impact the loose-tight leadership model had on processes that enhanced decision making and actual task performance as well as motivational related variables such as goal commitment, self-efficacy, and leader-follower mutual trust.

Thus as a leader, you are to be both directive *and* facilitative. You are to be tight at times, guiding what must get done, and loose at times, allowing others to decide how it gets done within certain defined quality parameters. How do you know what to be tight about and loose about? In professional learning community leadership, you get "tight" about the "right thing" components of your shared vision, and then you turn the vision into action by being "loose" with how the vision is accomplished by those responsible for the implementation.

At Stevenson, for example, we had committed ourselves to implementing student-engaged learning through reorganization of the classroom structure. Seven teachers, including me, ran a pilot in three different classrooms. We used a model called "teams of four," a classroom design that eliminated the use of rows except in testing situations. In hindsight, our decision to embrace the vision of student-engaged learning in the classroom through a blend of direct instruction and student participatory small-group instruction was a microcosm of the loose-tight leadership model for adults. At the teacher-student classroom level, we were trying to provide students a greater voice in their learning and a chance to "own" the classroom work. The teacher (leader) was being asked not to be just tight (to direct all the learning as the students stay respectfully muted), and not to be just loose (to set students up in teams of four and let chaos reign), but rather to use the best of both the loose and tight instructional strategies.

It was in the context of this highly effective classroom model that I first began to understand loose-tight as an organizational leadership model for my work as a school administrator. The teams of four classroom structure and my demand for the elimination of rows were watershed examples of this for me. What is it for you? Can you name that vision action that you personally care so much about that it moves you to an active response when you monitor? Can you ever recall thinking something like the following?

> *We will be tight about this "right thing." No choice. And we will implement this in our school or program area of my leadership. No options. No exceptions. However, we will be loose about how it gets implemented by each team of adults. We will work together and use our collective expertise to determine*

*many ways to get this "right thing" vision action done. We will take risks. We will constantly evaluate what is and is not working, and we will take action.*

By now you know what the "right thing" behavior was for me. What is the "right thing" behavior for which you cannot tolerate anything less than full implementation?

# Rejecting the Laissez-Faire Stance

In August 1993, I stood in front of the mathematics and science faculty on opening day (vision day) and stated:

> *It is time for our mathematics and science division of the school to take action on the districtwide vision of student-engaged learning. The time to act is now. This year. No option. Not a choice. Based on a pilot by seven teachers last year, based on the best we know from research, based on what is being taught by our national organizations, based on what we have learned from one another (all trusted sources), we will no longer, again—ever—teach our students with the desks sitting in rows. We will use a blend of whole-group and small-group instruction each day.*

Pretty directive, wouldn't you say? Top-down tight leadership, right? I asked each of the pilot teachers to say a few words about how to do it well (the loose part), and then I asked, "Can anyone think of any educationally sound reason students should sit in rows other than on test days? Can anyone advocate for the continued use of rows?"

The room was silent. After a few moments, one mathematics teacher asked, "Do we have to do this? Is it required?"

It was a defining moment for me as a leader. My response would decide whether I was just a manager of my area of the school hoping for eventual vision implementation, or a leader willing to ensure that the vision of student-engaged learning as a coherent aspect of our daily lesson planning would be fulfilled—with no tolerance for anything less. John Kotter (1999) phrased it like this: "The person who thinks management is leadership will manage change, hence keeping it under control, but he or she will be unable to provide the stuff required to make larger and more difficult leaps" (p. 11).

I was ready to make a larger and more difficult leap. I was thinking: correct, there are no other options. How could we in good conscience defend a practice that was not effective? All courses. All teachers. Every day. How many pilots do we need to do to be convinced? To be certain? This was a very difficult leap for all of us. Sounds a bit tense, and for a while it was.

As a leader, I was beginning to understand that my job was to be tight about the things that really mattered and to be crystal clear about *why* they mattered. As a professional learning community leader you cannot afford to be laissez-faire about your work. If anything, you must be serious and passionate about the business of educating every child extremely well—even as it is done with a sense of compassion, humor, and grace. It is such a worthy cause of your life's work. It is what draws many people to our profession. *Inviting* faculty, staff, and colleagues to take action on the vision is significantly different from *declaring and ensuring* everyone will take action. This was much more than an invitation. No options, no excuses, no exceptions.

My response to the teacher was as follows:

> *Why wouldn't we want to teach using research-affirmed practice? Why wouldn't we want the benefit of improved student learning that results from students engaging with each other around meaningful work? Why wouldn't we want to work together to make this an essential element of every lesson? How should we explain to our parents, the school board, and the general school community that we do not wish to pursue best-practice, research-affirmed instruction?*

My response in this situation illustrates a very important distinction for you to communicate as a leader. The vision message I was being tight about, ultimately, was not "Use teams of four in the classroom." Teams of four was a management structure that would help us achieve the actual vision. The non-negotiable, no-need-for-debate vision element was *student-engaged learning*. Adhering to that action was not optional. Although teams of four was the structure chosen to achieve this vision initially, if teachers and PLC teacher teams were able to provide evidence of other structures that achieved the same vision of instruction—great.

Teams must have some autonomy for how they do the work—otherwise adult motivation will dissipate quickly. So be careful to distinguish between the actual vision and the structures for achieving the vision. In this case, however, the existing structure—the status quo of rows—was not a choice anymore. That era was over. What "era" needs to be over for your program or area of school leadership?

# Knowing What Is and Is Not a "Choice"

Looking back, I had given teacher use of rows as a teaching and learning structure seven years to work. *Seven years!* Given the *choice* as to whether or not our faculty and staff should implement the vision of student-engaged learning, over seven years, several of those within the sphere of my influence made the choice *not to implement* the value. My only regret is that my initial tolerance level for implementation of this vision action was so high. I had waited too long as a leader to act decisively on this vital issue for improved student achievement. Within two years of required action on this vision element, our D and F rate in mathematics and science in all courses dropped by double-digit percentages. Several dropped to as low as 15–18 percent and reached all-time lows in the history of our school *immediately*. By 2002, our districtwide D and F rate in mathematics and science— all courses at all levels—had dropped below 9 percent. There may have been other correlated causes, but small steps taken toward student-engaged learning instruction and the hard work of the collaborative teacher learning teams to determine lesson plan solutions *together* were a major aspect of the improved student results.

My lengthy toleration of the choice *not* to implement student-engaged learning revealed something about me as a leader. Initially, I was not very well trained on the idea of a loose-tight model. To be that tight about something ("We will no longer teach using rows") requires the leader to provide greater clarity that it is a "right thing." I had to demonstrate that I understood the details and questions that could cause confusion as teachers attempted to implement the required changes. Achieving clarity also meant that as long as the spirit of the purpose behind teams of four was being honored (student-engaged learning), then teams of teachers should have significant freedom of choice and ownership about how to get it done well (loose, facilitative leadership with autonomy on the implementation side). The choice for how to implement student-engaged learning could be loose. However, *whether* to embrace student-engaged learning and implement this vision value was *not a stakeholder choice* anymore—not a choice of the students, parents, teachers, leaders, or fellow administrators. No need for debate. At some point you must lead the organization into full implementation of the vision. Otherwise, why are you leading?

When the leader exhibits tolerance of seeing the vision and values as a choice, then chaos reigns, accountability becomes random happenstance, variance and inequity become common, celebration becomes less focused and empty, and the "direction" of the work is lost. You can certainly display tolerance on the things that are loose—the actual methods or actions chosen to implement the vision and values. But there can be little or almost no tolerance of adult actions that do not advance the shared vision aspirations.

Professional learning community leaders are courageous in their dogged pursuit of the loose-tight implementation of the vision and values of the school or district. They clearly understand what is and isn't a decision-making choice for the variety of stakeholders in the school organization. In the end, parents, students, teachers, and administrators are *all* accountable for student-engaged learning and all other aspects of the shared school vision. Ultimately, your advanced skill in this discipline allows you to set boundaries on adult behaviors and actions, to support and defend autonomous movement within those boundaries, and to do so with grace and compassion.

# Defining Autonomy and Defending Boundaries

Robert Marzano and Timothy Waters, in *District Leadership That Works*, reveal a parallel finding to loose-tight leadership:

> How can we find school autonomy positively correlated with student achievement and site-based management exhibiting a negligible or negative correlation with achievement? The question might be answered in light of our other findings . . . *Defined autonomy* means that the superintendent expects building principals and all other administrators in the district to lead *within the boundaries defined by the district goals.* (2009, p. 8, emphasis in the original)

Understanding what is meant by "within the boundaries defined by the district goals" is an important and critical skill for the leadership discipline of accountability and celebration. As a PLC leader, you must become a boundary defender. The boundaries defined by the *district* vision and goals establish the most critical and coherent work of each school site in the district. Similarly, the boundaries defined by the *school* vision and goals should be in direct alignment with the district goals and define the most critical and common work of each grade level, department, or teacher team. These boundaries are tight, they are defined, they are non-negotiable, and yes, they are required.

Further, Marzano and Waters (2009) show that the defined autonomy boundaries *lower variance and increase the reliability* of adult actions that improve student achievement. That is exactly the goal of a professional learning community: high reliability and low variance in the quality of the teaching, learning, and assessing of every student. This goal is achieved because "effective leadership at the district and school levels changes what occurs in classrooms, and what happens in classrooms has a direct effect on student achievement" (Marzano & Waters, 2009, p. 11). The boundaries thus become what I call an inequity eraser from school to school, grade level to grade level, or teacher to teacher.

To visualize this idea, think of the box in figure 2.1 as a vision and values boundary box. The box represents adult behavior and actions that, although somewhat loose, must stay within the boundaries of the defined vision components.

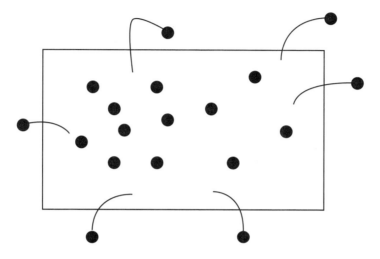

**Figure 2.1: Adult behaviors within the vision and values boundary box.**

*Visit **go.solution-tree.com/plcbooks** to download a reproducible version of this figure.*

Establishing boundaries and ensuring adherence to those boundaries can be stressful. The leader must identify these behaviors and actions.

Consider the vision and value of student-engaged learning. Do faculty members or administrators have the right to fly outside the student-engaged learning vision and values boundary and *not* actively engage students? Absolutely not. In fact, you and those you lead have an ethical, professional, and moral obligation to ensure the shared vision is implemented. Those you lead cannot fly outside of the box of the expected shared vision components. However, those individuals could use many different structures or methods to implement actions that serve the vision. How to implement the vision can and should be loose. As the leader you must give the faculty and staff autonomy within defined and well-articulated boundaries.

Paul Sullivan, in his 2010 book *Clutch*, indicates that one way to eliminate the stress in making clutch decisions is to provide parameters that focus the decision-making process. Essentially, the parameters (or boundaries) provide the focus needed to meet the targets for student achievement in a PLC. This is the wonderful paradox of the loose-tight or "defined autonomy" leadership culture. It is another of those leadership practices where the "tyranny of OR" (Collins & Porras, 1997, p. 43) cannot rule. Adults can work within a defined set of behaviors *and* have an opportunity for freedom and choice.

Autonomy is different from independence. Autonomy in the loose-tight PLC world does not mean the individualism of going it alone, relying on nobody. Yet as Daniel Pink (2009) points out, autonomy "means acting with choice—which means we can be both autonomous and happily interdependent with others. A sense of autonomy has a powerful effect on individual performance and attitude" (p. 90). This research-affirmed concept also extends to organizations and teams where leaders provide autonomy support to others. This might very well explain the Marzano-Waters paradox regarding site-based management (see quote at the beginning of this section, page 46).

Interestingly, according to Pink (2009), the autonomy workers seek is not necessarily over aspects of the vision—the stuff you must be tight about—but over four specific aspects of their work: "what they do, when they do it, how they do it, and whom they do it with" (pp. 93–94). These are the areas in which a PLC leader can be a bit loose.

What does this mean for you as a PLC leader? How can you be tight about vision implementation and give those you lead—those in your sphere of influence—a sense of well-defined autonomy and control?

- **What you do.** What you are to do in a PLC is defined by both the vision of curriculum, instruction, and assessment that has been developed by the district, school, or team, *and* the PLC expectations for team participation and team-based plans that turn the vision into action. "What you do" is developed and created during the action plan process that designs the work of the faculty and administration at the start of any school year. Autonomy is built in when you have established an ongoing yearlong process that allows all faculty and staff a voice in those required adult actions for the school year. That voice, however, is not a *we get to do whatever we want* voice. It is a voice defined within the parameters of the vision. As the leader, you must monitor that voice and ensure those parameters are being honored.

- **When they do it.** Education by its very nature is built around firm time schedules. Most school leaders enjoy the freedom to vary their schedule every day—within the constraints of being in an office or on a campus. The question for you to ask is this: are there ways (within reason) to provide some faculty control over when they do certain aspects of their job—especially the opportunity and time to engage with their professional learning community teams?

- **How they do it.** I have long been a champion of allowing faculty and staff teams to have a lot of freedom and choice over how to proceed as long as it meets the expectations of the district or school vision. This freedom is part of professional risk taking—inquiry-based efforts intended to figure out what works and doesn't work. Teams of adults cannot be afraid or worried about what will happen if a new idea they decide to try is not working. One way to feel more comfortable with autonomy over how to get things done is to make sure that every risk-taking action is tied back to some aspect of student growth and learning achievement, and then evaluating that action based on actual results and improvement throughout the school year.

- **Whom they do it with.** This is one of the most underapplied aspects of PLC leadership. Well-intentioned PLC leaders understand the necessity for teaching assignments that take into account teacher pedagogical knowledge *and* teacher relational competency. Possible assignments at the school or team level are made based on the leader's understanding and expectations for how well a specific set of adults will actually work and engage together in their PLC teams. In establishing team assignments (whether by grade level or course), the PLC leader attempts to create the best assignments based on pedagogical and content knowledge, as well as teacher relational competency—knowledge and strength in working with others.

Judith Warren Little and Lora Bartlett's (2010) research review indicates professional development with a sustained focus on subject-specific teaching—strongly tied to the curriculum, instruction, and assessment that students would encounter—produces the most consistent effect on subject teaching and student learning. They indicate that other professional development emphases, such as using hands-on activities, taking steps to increase gender equity, or preparing teachers for leadership roles, respond to widespread interests and concerns. Yet none of these shows a consistent relationship to teachers' conceptions of subject teaching or reported practices of subject teaching. Only the professional development focused on subject knowledge for teaching does so.

For this type of subject-knowledge professional development to take place (a boundary on *what* we are to do), careful consideration must be given to how various teacher teams are designed and brought together based on their ability to work well with one another (their character), their depth of experience with the content (competence), and their passion for the grade level or course (commitment). *Whom I work with* matters to the faculty and staff. And it should matter to you, if you hope to achieve greater success toward the goal of accountability and celebration, as you'll learn later when we examine lateral (peer) accountability (page 57).

Over the years, I learned to place faculty members on various teams based on relational *character* first, pedagogical *competence* second, and *commitment* to the cause third. Character, competence, commitment—in that order. Every time I placed someone on the team primarily because of competence, it caused a problem for that team if that person was not relationally a good match. More often than not, with the right match of relational skills, the team will help the competencies of each faculty or staff member to grow and be sustained over time. I learned this valuable lesson from a leadership mentor outside of education who had wisdom and success beyond my years and experience.

What happens when certain adults or students fly outside of the vision and values boundaries defined by the district, the school, or the agreed-upon team actions? What happens when certain adults act in ways contrary to the declared vision and values? Who holds others accountable? Who reigns in the diffusion and chaos caused by the randomness of actions outside of the defined boundaries? Are you, as a leader, prepared for this possibility? It always happens—every school year. And when it does—when vision actions "leak"—everyone is watching what you choose or do not choose to do. This is the place where your leadership credibility is formed. How will you respond?

# Turning Vision Into Action

The questions, then, for every PLC leader are these: How do you close your personal *turning vision into action* gap? How do you become a drift-resistant leader?

Can you think of a specific example or task in the past two years in which not just a few stakeholders but almost every adult stakeholder worked hard to implement a specific aspect of the current vision for your area of school leadership? Perhaps it was related to writing or reading across the curriculum, formative assessments with standards-based grading, response to intervention (RTI) structures for academic support, the use of integrated technologies for student and adult learning in elementary school classrooms, creative solutions for student placement into more rigorous courses or grade levels of study, or the expansion of support programs for the social and emotional development of children. Can you name it? What was the energy in your school like during that time? I imagine there was a lot of energy as well as inertia for implementation of the task.

Many leadership practices can provide the impetus for moving vision into action. Here is my list of the top eight practices. Answers to these questions about your personal leadership of a vision expectation provide a focus to specific steps you can take to support sustainability and momentum toward implementation of the desired vision. (Visit **go.solution-tree.com/plcbooks** to download a reproducible worksheet, *Moving Vision Into Action*, containing these questions.)

1. Do you *frequently* explain to those responsible for implementation the rationale for the vision action or behavior—why is this task or behavior so critical?

2. Do you allow those responsible for implementation the freedom (autonomy) to determine how to best accomplish the vision action or behavior within certain defined parameters? If so, what are those parameters?

3. Do you connect the vision action to measurable data (results) that you expect to improve because of the vision action or behavior? What are those data?

4. Do you ensure those adults responsible for implementation set short-term "targets that beckon" or SMART goals for specific improvement, evidenced by data and tied to the vision action or adult behavior? (SMART = **S**trategic & **S**pecific, **M**easurable, **A**ttainable, **R**esults oriented, and **T**ime bound; Conzemius & O'Neill, 2002)

5. Do you monitor and coach the expected vision action step or behavior for actual implementation on a weekly or monthly basis—if not more often?

6. Do you respond to your monitoring of the vision action by *celebrating*, frequently, those adult actions that led to implementation progress?

7. Do you respond to your monitoring of the vision action or behavior by providing *immediate, specific, and corrective feedback* to those adults not taking implementation action? Do you exhibit *low tolerance* with grace?

8. Do you clearly and regularly communicate to those you lead the non-negotiable aspect of the vision action or vital adult behavior? How do you do this?

This kind of close review of any vision action or vital behavior that you are working on will reveal whether it is fully implemented or not so fully implemented. The more yes answers you have—or at least greater degrees of yes—the more likely your leadership has set in motion the cultural conditions for full implementation. As the leader, you have a primary and profound influence over these factors. If you have a lot of no or "I'm not sure" answers, your chances of full implementation for the vision action step will be pretty low. These eight questions provide deeper insight into the factors that determine the size of the gap between your aspirations for vision action and your willingness to tolerate impediments to implementing the vision. Leaders who act decisively and teach with confidence, grace, and understanding can enable those they lead to respond in kind.

Regardless of your program or area of school leadership, one of your primary responsibilities is to develop and enforce an enduring, unending cycle of continuous improvement; a cycle of adult and student learning that again and again and again supports a culture of celebration and accountability to adult actions that will improve student learning; a cycle of proactive growth that will not wait for your school or program of school leadership to decline so far that the problems become easy to diagnose but too far gone to cure quickly.

In *How the Mighty Fall*, Jim Collins (2009) provides wisdom about how to prevent the natural decline that assaults most organizations, including school organizations. As he points out, the level of stagnation or decline that your area of school leadership will experience over time is largely self-inflicted. He states: "Failure is not so much a physical state as a state of mind; success is falling down, and getting up one more time, without end" (p. 123). In this respect, the pursuits of a PLC leader might best be described as *pick yourself up, dust yourself off, and start all over again.* In professional learning community school cultures, decline must be detected early and often and be immediately addressed by all levels of stakeholders. It is through the development of a cycle of accountability and celebration that the PLC leader turns vision into action and puts the brakes on possible decline. What is at stake with this leadership discipline is the opportunity to lead focused organizational change that eliminates status quo and "blame game" thinking in favor of continuous improvement, double-loop learning, and targets that beckon. In short, you want to engender an environment that favors vision speak over victim speak.

# Rejecting Victim Speak

Moving others to action, then, becomes an intentional leadership practice. The work in this leadership discipline begins with self-assessing your personal current reality. Are you taking action, or are you using victim speak? There is no neutral ground. Ask yourself, who is going to hold everyone accountable to engagement in and sustained action for the agreed-upon vision and values, and within the defined boundaries of expected action? In reflecting on this question, and in asking others to reflect on it, leaders move their school culture away from a *blaming others* "mindset" toward systemic and effective self-ownership at every level. Two to three years from now, you will be incomparably better at turning a well-developed vision of the school or area of the school program you lead into an *implemented reality*. You will close your own personal aspirations-tolerance gap, and so will those you lead and influence.

In 1983, there was no boundary on how much content I would or could teach in Algebra I by the end of the year. I could be three chapters or units ahead or behind other teachers, regardless of scope or depth of what was taught. Once the vision of a tightly aligned curriculum was established in our school, it was not my option to keep teaching as much or as little as I wanted during the year. But who was going to hold me accountable to this essential vision and value expectation? Me? My colleagues? My principal? My community?

By 1993, instruction had changed. Our teams of four model was implemented to fulfill the vision of student-engaged learning: every student would experience student-engaged learning and small-step instruction every day. This was a non-negotiable tight boundary on adult and student classroom behavior. But implementers (in this case teachers and students) had "loose from within" autonomy; they had autonomy to figure out what worked best and how to best get it done. Teachers and teacher teams decided *how* to best achieve the vision of student-engaged learning. Although very empowering for those closest to the action of student learning, the teams of four model also increased responsibility. And yet again, the question arose: *who was going to hold everyone accountable* to the engagement and sustained action for this vision and values boundary?

Similarly, in 2007, every teacher and leadership team in our district was required to submit and use a formative assessment action plan as part of the teacher and student learning process. Did every team *really* have to do it? In a professional learning community, who holds everyone accountable to the engagement and sustained action for this or any other vision and values boundary?

As described earlier, accountability and celebration relate to both the outcomes (improved student achievement) and the responsibility *to take actions* that will lead to those outcomes. Accountability requires freedom to make judgments and decisions within the boundary of expected behaviors. Any stakeholder—student, parent, teacher, administrator, or other school leader—who fails to take responsibility to implement actions that help fulfill the desired student achievement outcomes causes the gap to widen. Victim speak—statements that suggest it's someone else's fault that children are falling behind—is a dangerous aspect of how adults communicate with one another and can be toxic to the school culture. If allowed to go unchecked by the leaders, victim speak becomes part of a "staged disease" as referenced by Collins in the opening epigraph (page 35).

It is useful here to review the definition of the discipline of accountability and celebration:

> **The leadership work of delivering specific improvement in student achievement results and monitoring stakeholder actions that lead to those results, with consequences**

If we play the blame game and act like victims, a vicious cycle of finger-pointing results. Parents blame everything that goes wrong on the teacher or school principal (even though at best, teachers have students for only half the days of a year, and one-third of each day.) The school faculty and administration, in turn, blame the parents: if the parents would just step up to the plate and take responsibility to teach values and provide good nutrition, emotional support, and encouragement to do well, then students could really learn. Teachers, meanwhile, blame things that go wrong on the students or the administration: if our principal would just support our effort and appreciate us more, and if students would just work harder, try harder, be more positive, show up more often, develop mature habits, and take responsibility without error, then everything would be fine.

If victim speak dominates your stakeholder communication, you will never bridge the gap between realization of your aspirations and your tolerance for impediments to implementing the vision. If victim speak is allowed to dominate your school culture, negative values and beliefs create an "if only" conditional culture to student learning and success: *if only* our school had a decent principal; *if only* our school had better teachers; *if only* our students would do their homework; *if only* our students would attend school; *if only* we didn't have to worry about state tests; *if only* our parents really cared; *if only* others would do their jobs right; *then* we could have a great school and take meaningful action. In such an environment, the hope and promise that your leadership will make things better erodes quickly.

How do we avoid the "if onlys"? How do we avoid a cycle of blame? How do we engage our stakeholders into taking action and moving beyond asking, who is going to hold me accountable to this?

The answer lies partially in the quality of the ongoing accountability and celebration system taught and monitored by the leader—a system designed to prevent the natural disease of program stagnation and decline, a system designed to detect the disease early and provide a quick but effective cure, a system designed to foster movement of teams through three tiers of accountability and celebration: self, lateral, and vertical. Such a system strengthens the development and enforcement of an enduring cycle of continuous improvement.

## Understanding Tiers of Accountability

As a general rule, people do want to act with responsibility for the right things. And we especially want encouragement when we act with responsibility. However, it is often easier for us to see and judge the accountability and celebration actions (or lack thereof) of others rather than those of ourselves. The well-disciplined PLC leader understands that the role of *who* in the accountability and celebration discipline is stewardship for what we will become, and the *who* is *everyone*. In healthy professional learning communities, everyone becomes a steward of the vision, and the leader must help everyone make the decision to become a steward. As Pink (2009) comments, "This era doesn't call for better management. It calls for a renaissance of self-direction" (p. xi).

When you recognize and support three tiers of personal accountability—or responsibility to action—the school culture will flourish toward the expected vision. Figure 2.2 (page 56) shows the three tiers, which move from vertical accountability at tier 3, to lateral accountability at tier 2, to self-accountability at tier 1. One of the goals of the PLC leader's life is to move as many adults (and eventually students) to the first and second tier of accountability.

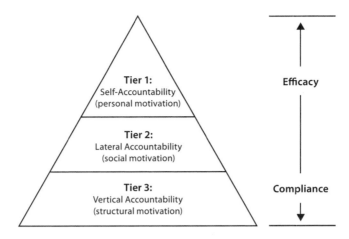

**Figure 2.2: Tiers of accountability and celebration to vision action.**

Visit **go.solution-tree.com/plcbooks** to download a reproducible version of this figure.

The tiers of accountability and celebration to vision action must be built on a foundation of vertical accountability established by you. As a leader, you are responsible, ultimately, for ensuring that the vision is solidified and action is underway to implement it. Your acceptance of personal accountability is crucial at the outset because it ensures that your model will be in place to support continuous improvement and the PLC expectation for a culture of lateral and self-accountability.

As those you lead begin to function in tiers 1 and 2, accountability will eventually become a more positive aspect of the school culture. Those closest to the action—classroom teachers—will become more autonomous, committed rather than merely compliant, and will take control of vision implementation.

## Tier 1: Self-Accountability and Celebration

Ultimately, your task as a professional learning community leader is to develop and nurture in others the best kind of accountability—self-accountability, the willingness to look in the mirror and ask, what more can I do to fulfill our school vision? After all, every stakeholder is accountable to carry out the vision of the school and program. As discussed earlier, stakeholders are more likely to assume this responsibility readily when the hard work of vision development has been a shared effort from the beginning.

Self-accountability is the cornerstone of school ethics and professionalism—and it is hard. It is who you are and what you do when no one is watching. When you have a well-developed sense of self-accountability, you are honest with yourself, and you are willing to be answerable for your actions and student results to your peers and others.

One way to measure whether or not there are high levels of self-accountability in those you lead is to do a quick monitoring check of their daily behavior and actions. Over the course of a week, notice the verbal behaviors of those you lead—five or more colleagues. What do you notice about the exact words they use to describe the causes of and responses to problems, issues, and concerns? If you were to place those words into two columns, one for self-accountability and one for victim speak, which column would have the most entries? More importantly, do you notice a pattern of victim speak that dominates each person you observe?

I do this activity every time I enter a school building. It is a way for me to quickly know if a culture of self-accountability has yielded to a culture of blaming others or circumstances (barrier thinking).

## Tier 2: Lateral Accountability and Celebration

In a professional learning community, the next tier of accountability is the social accountability of your personal group or team. Michael Fullan (2001) captures this understanding in the term *lateral accountability*. He further states:

> In hierarchical systems, it is easy to get away with superficial compliance or even subtle sabotage. In the interactive system I have been describing, it is impossible to get away with not being noticed (similarly, good work is more easily recognized and celebrated). There is, in fact, a great deal of peer pressure along with peer support in collaborative organizations. If people are not contributing to solutions, their inaction is more likely to stand out. The critical appraisal in such systems, whether it be in relation to the performance of a peer or the quality of an idea, is powerful. (p. 188)

Fullan's keen insight hints at the fact that without consequences, positive and negative, *accountability* is an empty term. The concept of holding someone accountable should enter into the peer social experience. As an example, suppose learning team members work together and decide to integrate a specific technology into a student project. The project becomes an agreed-upon team action. What happens when an individual team member decides *not* to integrate the technology into his or her teaching? How will the team choose to address this lack of self-accountability and the resulting inequity for this teacher's students? Will a peer from the team say to this teacher, "We will be responsible for the right things together, and you must ensure your students experience this technology as well?"

Lateral accountability, when correctly applied, creates a built-in and healthy peer pressure in response to individual teacher actions. Every learning team in your school or district should exert on its members a certain pressure and accountability to action that serve the vision of the school and the team.

## Tier 3: Vertical Accountability and Celebration

Although tier 3 is not the ideal level for accountability, at times it is required. Especially in the beginning of a cultural change, the PLC leader must be willing to be the final defender of accountability and celebration regarding the expectation to take action on the vision—for every team and for all of the individual faculty and staff. In a well-defined accountability system, your willingness to ensure the vision sticks and turns into action is paramount. Otherwise, random activity will rule the day, and faculty and administration will drift away from self-accountability. Your leadership strength in upholding the bottom line on vital behaviors and actions for the vision will prevent deep organizational decline and will foster more lateral and self-accountability.

Ultimately, accountability is *not* conditional. If consequences for lack of action or poor results don't result from self-motivation or from the social motivation of peers, then the leader must have the courage to once again explicitly design structures of behavior (like teams of four) that help to define what each person is responsible *to do and achieve.* Vertical accountability occurs when you, as the PLC leader, make it clear that implementation of the agreed-upon vital adult behavior is not a choice. I call this the Ronnie Lott rule. Ronnie Lott was a famous defensive back with the San Francisco 49ers. When he joined the 49ers, he was a renegade with no desire to follow the 49ers' vision. But his fellow defensive backs held him accountable to the expected behaviors of the team. If they hadn't, the defensive coach would have. If Lott still hadn't adapted to the vision for the team at that point, everyone on the team knew that ultimately, head coach Bill Walsh would use vertical accountability structures. But ideally, that vertical accountability would never be necessary, because his peers helped him to adjust.

The expression *with consequences* that is part of the definition of this discipline conveys the theme of accountability that is central to maintaining continuous improvement, and it is often difficult for many adults working in the school to accept. The need for an accountability and celebration system is beyond question, however, and consequences are not optional, either. Accountability and celebration are fundamental to the leadership of the vision, and you cannot abdicate that responsibility. Instead, you must ask the critical questions: Do we have a knock-your-socks-off sense of self-efficacy? Do we have an effective accountability and celebration system that constantly seeks improvement while checking for signs of decline?

Ultimately, vertical accountability works both ways. It is a reciprocal path and part of what Wilfred Drath (2001) calls relational dialogue. Accountability does not reside in a person or in a title as much as it does in the social and collaborative system of the professional learning community. As collaborative thought and action become the predominant model to achieve the school's vision, the tiers of accountability and celebration become blurred and blended. It does not matter so much where the locus of accountability and celebration begins and ends. What matters is that it is a vibrant aspect of the school culture.

The best accountability systems provide enough autonomy that most of those you lead begin to exhibit tier 1 and tier 2 behaviors over time as part of their relational response within the professional learning community. In these systems, the three tiers interact fluidly and regularly celebrate implementation of the vision.

# Leading a Well-Designed System for Monitoring Continuous Improvement

The journey of growth in this leadership discipline requires you to develop a system that turns vision into action and sustains continuous improvement and growth—forever. As a leader, how do you create an "early detection" process for change and growth that first and foremost creates built-in accountability to and celebration of results, yet also feeds the need for adult autonomy? Second, how do you create a system that preserves the values of the vision, yet advances risk-taking actions that implement those values?

The key word is *system*. As a leader you must institute an accountability and celebration system that supports all faculty, staff, and administrative routines and actions throughout your area of school leadership. Of course, it is true that you work to preserve the values of the vision—your agreed-upon and declared right things. But values merely describe a better future. To actually achieve that better future requires that you lead the organization through *cycles of formative learning and growth*. The frequency of these cycles varies according to school organizational levels—the district, the school, and the classroom. All these institutions contribute to implementing the vision and sustaining continuous improvement. Figure 2.3 presents a model for this cycle for monitoring continuous improvement toward the vision.

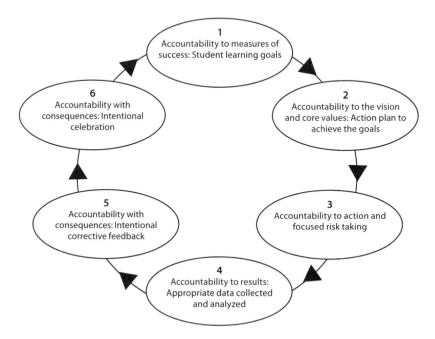

**Level 1:** *A district collaborative cycle of continuous improvement for all programs led by district leaders*

**Level 2:** *A school-site collaborative cycle of continuous improvement led by the principal and school-site leaders*

**Level 3:** *Grade-level or course-based team collaborative cycles of improvement at the grassroots level of student impact led by teacher teams and team leaders*

*The deeper the level (the closer to the classroom and students), the more frequently the cycle should repeat.*

**Figure 2.3: The accountability and celebration model for continuous improvement.**

*Visit* **go.solution-tree.com/plcbooks** *to download a reproducible version of this figure.*

At a minimum a systematic analysis of improvement should occur on a yearly or semester basis at the school-site level. Think of it as a detection process for potential elements of malaise and decline that asks, how well is our vision being implemented? At the teacher-team level, the cycle can occur more frequently, on a week-to-week or unit-by-unit basis following normal curriculum, instruction, and assessment implementation guidelines. The deeper the level (the closer to the classroom and students), the more frequently the cycle should repeat.

Within each of these organizational levels, the same criteria for accountability and celebration for continuous improvement apply. These criteria provide credibility for the district leader as an organizational change agent at the school level, for a school leader to become an organizational change agent at the teacher team level, and for a teacher to become a change agent for student learning. These criteria are described in the next section of this chapter, which addresses the six stages of the continuous improvement model in detail.

This approach to continuous improvement provides the PLC leader with a systemic process for turning the organizational vision into implemented practice. The model provides a sound and strong system of support and pressure—of *celebration and accountability*. This system:

1. Distributes accountability among all adults and provides clear expectations for responsibility to action item implementation

2. Optimizes conditions and resources for noticing adult behaviors in the school and leads to greater faculty empowerment, self-efficacy, and low tolerance for adult behaviors inconsistent with the vision

3. Promotes the ongoing and reflective use of data to meet school and community expectations and to determine if the work of the teams is making a difference

4. Builds a learning community culture of ongoing planning, reflection, evaluation, implementation, and goal setting—defined and collective autonomy

5. Supports focused risk-taking adult actions on ideas that will help the school achieve the vision of improved student achievement

In this model, the system—with the support of the leader—does the heavy lifting of turning vision into action. Remember, the voice of authority for the coherent focus of the school's work does not ask *who*. The voice of authority reinforces the vision—the *what* you are to become. As a leader, it is your job to ensure the vision's voice of authority is heard and paid attention to by all stakeholders, hopefully at a tier 1 or tier 2 level of accountability.

This model of continuous growth and improvement is built in such a way as to sustain long-term success in implementing the vision even as school leaders transition in and out of positions over time. The model provides an opportunity to keep a sustained, consistent vision focus over a period of three to five years, while changing operating practices and strategies to improve upon the vision components during each cycle of growth.

# Implementing the Continuous Improvement Model

How do you get started with the continuous improvement model? Remember, we have two areas of accountability as a school: accountability to actions and accountability to results. Both are essential. But where should you start—action planning or results planning? In many instances, schools and school programs start with action planning as a way to get traction and momentum. *It is a mistake to start there.*

Starting with action planning causes both ownership issues and evidence of success issues for the leader. For example, suppose a superintendent, central office curriculum director, or school principal requires teacher professional development on—and expects subsequent implementation of—a new school literacy program. Two issues immediately surface for the school leader:

1. Who are the *owners* of the implementation action(s)? Did those closest to the action have a voice in the expected literacy actions that will result from the professional development? Exactly which part of the school's vision components will be met if all adults implement this action? Has the action of adopting a literacy program been connected to the school or district vision? Is that connection well understood by the faculty and staff?

2. How exactly will this action be *measured for success?* What student achievement results are expected to improve if this action is implemented?

It is difficult to exercise your tier 3 vertical accountability as the leader if you have not answered these two questions first.

For this reason, it's best to plan for accountability to results first, and align action plans accordingly. This process begins with establishing criteria for accountability and celebration, criteria that can be evaluated formatively at the district, school, and classroom levels. In the continuous improvement model, these criteria for accountability to results are aligned with six stages of planning and implementation.

Stage 1:   Set student learning goals (accountability to measures of student success)

Stage 2:   Create an action plan to achieve the goals (accountability to the vision and values)

Stage 3:   Take action on what works and what is best for students (accountability to action and focused risk taking)

Stage 4:   Collect and analyze appropriate data (accountability to results)

Stage 5:   Provide intentional corrective feedback (accountability with consequences)

Stage 6:   Provide intentional celebration (accountability with consequences)

In an effective continuous improvement model, ideas such as the literacy program mentioned earlier are never implemented on an ad hoc basis. Rather, student learning goals are determined first, in Stage 1, and the appropriate action plans to meet those achievement goals—which may or may not include a literacy program—are developed in response in Stage 2. Teachers and teacher teams implement the plans in Stage 3, collect data on the results in Stage 4, adjust the action plans according to the data in Stage 5, and celebrate their progress toward the goals in Stage 6. Along the way, the PLC leader monitors and supports the teams at every stage, providing tier 3 vertical accountability as necessary, and celebrating their progress and actions whenever possible.

## *Stage 1: Set Student Learning Goals*

Perhaps the greatest void that school leaders desperately need to fill is the void caused by not knowing if you are making any authentic progress as a district, as a school, or as a program. Many educators work without ever knowing—or knowing in time—if their work really matters for that year, much less on a semester-by-semester or month-to-month basis. And that void often leaves many of the adults you lead feeling unmotivated and stagnant.

In the Harvard Business Review's *Breakthrough Ideas for 2010*, Teresa Amabile and Steven Kramer provide insight into "what really motivates workers." They highlight a multiyear study of workers and their immediate supervisors on employee motivation based on five factors: recognition, incentives, interpersonal support, support for making progress, and clear goals. The six hundred leaders surveyed were sure that by far the number-one motivational factor cited by workers would be "recognition for good work." And they were dead wrong. By far—on 76 percent of motivated workers' best days—workers said their number-one motivational factor was "making progress in one's work" (Amabile & Kramer, 2010, p. 2). The action message was clear. Leaders need to notice and celebrate progress toward goals—even incremental progress—above all else.

In schools, the most meaningful progress is in student learning. Therefore, Stage 1 of the continuous improvement cycle is to create accountability to measures of student success, and to do so, you must first define the measures of student success. Start by setting student learning goals that are what I've called "targets that beckon." Begin by collecting student achievement data: what are the data trends from previous years? Working collectively, use the data to set realistic goals for student achievement, participation rate, satisfaction, and discipline, as measured by local, state, and national benchmarks. These goals should be written, owned, and aligned for at least three levels of the school organization: the district leadership team, the school-site leadership team, and the grade-level or course-based teacher team. Effective leaders will ensure that every team defines measurable outcomes of progress toward the shared vision.

One way to accomplish Stage 1, setting student learning goals, is to use the SMART school teams model described by Anne Conzemius and Jan O'Neill in *The Handbook for SMART School Teams* (2002). In this model, district, school-site, and grade-level or course teacher teams discuss the previous year's trend data and examine specific areas of program weakness. At the district level, for example, a team SMART goal for students might be: "We will increase the percentage of students that meet or exceed standards on the state assessments from 62 percent to 75 percent by spring 2014." A school site goal might be: "We will increase the number of EL (English learner) students that meet or exceed standards on the state assessment at our school from 42 percent to 60 percent by spring 2014." A grade-level or subject-area teaching team might set this goal: "We will increase the number of third-grade students that meet or exceed reading standards from 70 percent to 88 percent by the spring of 2014."

In the cycle for continuous improvement, these results-driven goals set by each level (district, school, or grade or course team) are reviewed and revised by that level on a yearly basis each August (see fig. 2.3., page 60). Each level needs to write and own the designed goals for measurable improvement. At the grade level or teacher team–level, the progress or measurement goals should be written collaboratively with input from all faculty on that team. Notice how all of these measures of success given in this section are written as *we will* statements and can be designed to demonstrate growth toward greater degrees of success in student achievement, participation, satisfaction, or behavior by the end of a certain time period. The statements are used to create targets that beckon for short-term wins during the school year.

The student learning goals that are set in Stage 1 at the grade-level or course-based team, school site, or district level are foundational for the rest of the continuous improvement cycle.

## Stage 2: Create an Action Plan to Achieve the Goals

At Stage 2, the district team, the school site team, and the teacher grade-level or course-based team each work collaboratively to plan and develop *action steps* to reach the Stage 1 SMART goals for improved student learning in the specific course or program. The criterion for evaluating the work at this stage is accountability to the vision and values. Do the action steps align with and support the district vision and values?

During Stage 2 planning, teacher teams seek common ground for the work of the grade level or course during the school year. As part of this work, teachers may create and share common products, including warm-up problems, practice materials, grade-level unit exams, reviews for exams, writing and scoring rubrics, long- and short-term projects, homework expectations, new curriculum materials or instruction methods, methods of integrating technology, and motivational techniques.

Teachers may need your leadership guidance and teaching for how to create a good action plan. The well-trained PLC leader will ensure that his or her action plan components are aligned within acceptable boundaries that help achieve the vision and values. This planning can be somewhat loose in that great ideas in the plan can be generated from anywhere and vary widely. You can support the plans as long as you believe they will turn vision into action and improve results, as defined by the goals in Stage 1. However, as the leader, *you must monitor the plans* to ensure they are aligned with the vision of best practice. You must be willing to provide samples of model plans and, when necessary, ask some teams to rewrite their plans for better quality. You will need to provide oversight of Stages 1 and 2 at the start of the year and again at midyear. This monitoring is very important to your success as a leader in turning vision into the reality of action.

The work completed in Stage 1 and Stage 2 becomes the basis for authentic adult professional learning. Teachers can explore such questions as these:

- *Why should we take these actions?*

- *How do we know they will work?*

- *What happens if they don't work out?*

- *How do we try this?*

- *I have never taught with students in groups. Any suggestions?*

In the cycle of continuous improvement, the accomplishments in each stage contribute to the work of the next. For example, Stage 2's planning is important, because it will be expected in Stage 3 that *everyone* will carry out the plan. Taking action in Stage 3 and then analyzing data on the results of that action in Stage 4 will lead to moments of accountability in all three tiers—self, lateral, and vertical.

## Stage 3: Take Action on What Works and What Is Best for Students

As teams continue to meet weekly, teachers discuss what is and isn't working and which action steps from the Stage 2 plan make sense. In this stage, the criteria for evaluation are accountability to action and focused risk taking. Members hold one another accountable (lateral accountability) for taking the agreed-upon actions and implementing new plans with focused risk taking. For example, if the team decides a certain technology should be integrated into the curriculum, then *every team member must honor the agreed-upon action.* No options. Ideally, the team does not let a team member drift into bad habits, practices, or isolation from others. Realistically, the team leader, grade-level leader, curriculum director, instructional leader, department chair, or assistant principal or principal must be willing to step in and hold all team members accountable to the Stage 2 implementation plan.

For example, suppose a sophomore English team decides to use a specific homework makeup policy for all students in sophomore English as a way to meet the goals aligned with the school's vision for accurate student feedback, student responsibility, and teacher consistency with grade assignments. One team member decides not to use this policy and applies a more stringent policy. Her decision causes two problems. First, she is violating an agreed-upon team action that undermines the collective autonomy of the team. Second, her students will be graded differently than all other students in the course. How does a grade for the sophomore English course have meaning and accuracy if teachers do not apply consistent, equitable, and congruent assessment standards?

To resolve the problem, the team leader and fellow team members first communicate these questions and the expectations that the teacher will meet the agreed-upon team standard. This course of action reflects moving into a more rigorous form of lateral accountability and efficacy. If a teacher or an administrator fails to comply either independently or from the peer response of team members, then you—the leader—must be willing to intervene with a vertical accountability response. Tolerating anything less will undermine the success of lateral accountability for those you lead.

## A Note on Timely Monitoring

A leader well trained in the discipline of accountability and celebration knows that constant monthly monitoring is required during Stages 2 and 3 to ensure the right actions are planned and implemented. Your monitoring is a critical aspect of the cycle for improvement.

Failure to notice and monitor what is going on can be embarrassing. During the year I served my district as assistant superintendent, I carried the primary responsibility for leading the district-level continuous improvement plan. I successfully achieved Stages 1 and 2 of the cycle of continuous improvement, using our annual leadership retreat in August to establish our measurable data targets and our vision actions for the school year. I subsequently collaborated with various levels of our school leadership teams to complete a robust and thorough plan that met with board approval in September.

However, one critical leadership flaw emerged as the school year advanced and the business of our work consumed our days. *I failed to monitor* the plan to see if we were actually taking Stage 3 action on any of the components of our robust plan. I waited to examine actual implementation and action on the plan until it was time, in late spring, to present a report on results data collected and analyzed in Stage 4 and corrective actions outlined in Stage 5. At that moment in late spring—almost ten months later—I realized we had failed in almost every area of our school programs to carry out the agreed-upon district actions within the plan. My reports on Stage 4 and Stage 5 were moot, because we never took action in Stage 3. As the leader, I should have noticed our lack of action toward these critical vision components much sooner. In a very embarrassing and public way, I had to admit to my unhappy board of education that we had failed to carry out the plan created the previous September.

Running the leadership race sometimes has its hurdles—and its lessons learned. After that, every January we filed a midyear progress report that detailed progress on every aspect of our school programs during Stage 3—no more May surprises!

## Stage 4: Collect and Analyze Appropriate Data

The success of leading Stage 4 depends on establishing results-oriented goals in Stage 1 and outlining clear action plans for those goals in Stage 2—and, of course, implementing those plans in Stage 3. The criterion for evaluation at Stage 4 is accountability to results. To understand whether the team has shown accountability to results, members must first understand which data are relevant, how those data will be collected, and what action will be taken in response to the data (in Stage 5). Mike Schmoker (1999) supports this process when he states: "Concentrating on results does not negate the importance of action. On the contrary, the two are interdependent. Results, the moment revealed, tell us which actions are most effective and to what extent and where actions need reexamining and adjusting" (p. 4). As the leader, you use Stage 4 as an occasion to monitor and foster greater self-accountability. At this stage, ask:

- *Did the actions [assuming the actions actually took place] of the adults and students lead to improved results or not?*

- *Did we make progress on our goals or not?*

- *Did our work matter, in the sense that student learning increased, based on our chosen measures of success?*

- *Are we making progress toward our student achievement goals through our current vision and values actions?*

- *Before it is too late, what types of intervention can and should we provide?*

The Stage 3 actions are taken in hopes of achieving better results. Stage 4 ensures the right data are collected and provided as needed to measure *immediate* results, in order to inform our next actions—Stage 5 work.

## Stage 5: Provide Intentional Corrective Feedback

In this stage, working together, teams of teachers and administrators determine progress and provide feedback for either positive or negative consequences in an immediate, effective, nonjudgmental, and celebratory way. Your ability to lead with grace and teach others how to communicate with dignity is paramount. Through this analysis of the data, as members meet the criteria of accountability with consequences, a culture of candor takes shape.

Several factors are critical to success in leading Step 5:

1. Immediate and corrective feedback to the team is provided on results as well as actions. All target goals and results are shared immediately. Leaders also review Stage 2 action plans and provide feedback to the team, for discussion purposes, on its level of implementation.

2. Feedback from the tier 3 (vertical) level of accountability is provided for faculty and faculty teams in which tier 1 (self) and tier 2 (lateral) accountability measures were not sufficient to make progress toward goals and actions.

3. A reflective team response to the data provided is expected. This formative response for all adults serves to drive the future improvement of Stage 2 and Stage 3 plans and actions. This response is due to the leader within a week of the Stage 5 data reviews.

4. Time is allocated for Stage 5 corrective feedback and review by all teams at all levels. All faculty and administrative teams understand that specific feedback during the Stage 5 review process is crucial to their own growth and learning within the cycle of improvement.

5. A culture of candor and transparency exists at all levels of accountability and celebration of the results.

In Stage 5, a window of transparency about progress toward goals opens. In this moment, faculty and administrators often reach a collective sense of satisfaction about progress made—no matter how incremental—as well as a collective understanding of which specific actions worked well or not so well.

Stage 5 works best when teachers and teacher teams execute it with self-direction and self-accountability. Some of my favorite questions to ask at Stage 5 with teacher or administrative teams include the following:

- *What are we learning from these results and actions?*
- *How can we improve on these data for the next cycle of our work?*
- *Are we making progress toward our vision of a better future?*
- *What interventions do we need to consider for the next cycle of improvement?*
- *What specific areas of our curriculum are causing the students the most problems?*
- *How could we adjust our instruction and assessments?*

As a leader, you must ask these questions until you are satisfied with the answers you receive. This is the time for closing the gap between expectations and implementation. Your ultimate leadership goal, however, is for *every* team to eventually ask and answer these questions under its own leadership and direction.

## Stage 6: Provide Intentional Celebration

What is your radical plan for celebration? Intentional celebration is necessary in a school culture in which the expended effort of the adults will never be good enough. If a teacher team or administrative team does not meet its student learning goal, the team refocuses the plan for the next cycle. If a team does meet its student learning goal, the team members must set a higher goal. In a school serious about pursuing continuous improvement and forever avoiding decline for student learning, all adults—faculty and administrators—are never at rest.

However, the stress caused by this pursuit can be diminished with intentional and well-designed public and private celebrations. The criteria of accountability with consequences include accountability for *positive* consequences. You can and should celebrate a range of accomplishments: movement toward the vision and values, short-term wins created by meeting SMART goals, three- to five-year trend data that show improvement, individual and collective adult actions, and effort that shows taking ownership for improved results. Celebrations bring out the emotion of the human work experience and make the effort worthwhile.

Celebrating continuous improvement has the flywheel effect that Collins (2001) describes:

> When you let the flywheel do the talking, you don't need to fervently communicate your goals. People just extrapolate from the momentum of the flywheel for themselves. "Hey, if we just keep doing this, look where we can go!" As people decide to turn the fact of potential into the fact of results, the goal almost sets itself. (p. 177)

Stage 6 is not an optional aspect of continuous improvement. You must embrace the public celebration of student results and adult actions. Public recognition and reward—celebrating together—for movement on the continuous improvement wheel builds community and reinforces key values of your school or program culture. As individuals or teams are singled out at a public event, they serve as role models for their peers. Public celebration is essential and requires intentional planning—at all levels of the school organization.

# Spending the Human Capital of Encouragement

As Terrence Deal and M. K. Key (1998) state: "Celebrations infuse life with passion and purpose. They summon the human spirit" (p. 11). James Kouzes and Barry Posner (1999) indicate that adult performance increased when led by individuals who gave encouragement. Yet their studies also showed that when asked, "Do you need encouragement to perform at your best?" many respondents said no. They didn't *need* encouragement (almost a tier 1 self-accountability response), but they *wanted* encouragement. Encouragement, when the leader freely gave it, helped their performance reach a higher level.

Knowing this, why is it that, as leaders, we often fail to create and sustain a culture of celebration and ongoing encouragement? Why do we fail to take advantage of our most important capital for rewards—the human capital of encouragement? The discipline of celebration (as a positive consequence to action) is a tonic that alleviates the pressure of the PLC culture of continuous improvement—the relentless drive, always and forever, to improve.

Can you train to get better at celebration? Yes. Leaders can learn to do the following:

- Use celebrations to notice and reinforce adult actions that advance the vision and values (Stages 2 and 3).

- Use celebrations privately to help connect all faculty and staff to progress on short-term team goals.

- Use celebrations to build community and commitment to the vision and values.

- Use celebrations to publicly recognize achievement of improved student results and behaviors.

- Use celebrations to create a culture of encouragement—the leader's social capital.

Celebrating together in community is an essential part of a viable and healthy school culture as well as a primary attribute of a successful PLC. Something very valuable occurs in families, schools, and corporations when we bring people together for social support and celebrations. We promote the health and well-being of others and ourselves.

So, how do you approach celebration? What routine do you use on a day-in, day-out basis that quietly celebrates the work and remarkable effort of those in your sphere of influence? Do you have a plan? Does it come naturally to you—and is it sincere and authentic?

About three years into my tenure as a school leader, one of my staff members—Dolores—came running into my office one day and asked me if I was mad at her. I said no, why? She said, "Well, you left this note in my mailbox, and there was no smiley face!" I assured her that everything was fine and that I just had been in a hurry at the moment I left that note. Dolores had picked up on a very subtle but heartfelt aspect of my leadership—constant smiley faces on all of my notes. It was my way of recognizing that the tasks we had to do were hard, yet appreciated. I think it was a carryover from my days as a classroom teacher where I used lots of stickers and motivational tools with students. Adults also need encouragement, and a little encouragement boost goes a long way.

Early on, I began a weekly routine of writing two to three handwritten personal notes (no more than five or six lines) on a small card to various adults under my direct leadership. I had a long ride home each day, and on the ride home I would just ask myself, Whom haven't I noticed much lately, and what are they doing to help advance the vision and values of the school? I would make sure a short note was in their mailboxes the next day. This routine did not cost much more than ten or fifteen minutes of my time in the evening. Rarely did I receive an immediate response to these notes—but I wasn't writing them to get a response. I was writing them to reinforce the actions and values of those on my staff—and perhaps even encourage those struggling to meet the standards we were setting for the behavior of all adults. You become a person of influence when you demonstrate confidence in others and just flat-out expect and notice the best from them.

After more than twenty years of this routine, it was very typical for me to hear from retiring staff members about the impact those notes had on their careers. Some would even produce the five or six notes I had written to them (I always dated them) and would tell me that they often pulled them out and reread them on the tougher days, when they just needed a bit of a boost. Interestingly, the notes that also encouraged them to new action and what they saw as risk taking seemed to have the greatest impact.

In addition, every year at Thanksgiving I would write an open letter to the faculty and staff thanking them for their hard work, and creating a context for our progress to date for the school year. It just seemed to me that by Thanksgiving, the school year begins to take on a sort of life of its own. And so, in keeping with the theme of that season, it's a good time to be clear about our purpose and remind ourselves of the importance of our work. My only evidence of the impact of these yearly letters was the year I did not write one due to time constraints on my own schedule—when I didn't write the letter, I heard about it from quite a few folks. Needless to say, the following year, I was careful to plan for it in my work schedule.

What are you doing to encourage staff? What is your version of the smiley face, the private note, or the open letter of gratitude?

## The Tall Poppy Syndrome

Though I later came to value celebration, early in my leadership career, I was often the voice at our administrative table arguing against public celebration. It seemed to me we would invariably forget to mention someone who had accomplished something, and then feelings would be hurt. It also seemed to me that we had no rules for what would be celebrated. How would we know whom to celebrate? Would the rest of the staff really want to sit there while we celebrated the efforts of their colleagues who did things better than they did? This type of deficit thinking is sometimes known as the *tall poppy syndrome*—a pejorative term used to describe a social phenomenon in which people of genuine merit are resented, attacked, cut down, or criticized because their talents or achievements elevate them above or distinguish them from their peers. *But I was very wrong.*

Over the years, as we systemically began to think of celebration as an important aspect of our continuous growth as a school community, eventually all of us became taller poppies—and it had an impact on our students as well. As a school organization, our incremental pursuit of greatness was often best revealed during these celebration moments. We would reach critical milestones and ask, can we get taller? At Stevenson, this became a public event conducted three times during the year. We planned for public celebrations with all adults at the start of the year on opening day, during midyear between semesters, and at the end of the school year before the summer break. We shared and celebrated our trend data and student achievement data at the start of the year. We celebrated our student satisfaction data (student survey results) during midyear, and we celebrated our "Super Pats" (we were the Patriots) at midyear and the end of the year.

As principal, Dan Galloway would stand at the podium on our stage in the Performing Arts Center and, in front of more than five hundred school district faculty and staff, celebrate the accomplishments of many. His presence and sincere tone of voice caused everyone to focus and listen as he read story after story of celebration. For example, a typical story read to our faculty and staff was as follows:

> *When a colleague's spouse was critically ill for an extended period of time, these two teachers stepped in to help out in a big way. In their efforts to ensure that no student fell behind due to the extended absence of the teacher, these two individuals created sub plans, shared teaching responsibilities, wrote and scored assessments, and provided students with extra help as needed. Their superior efforts helped to minimize the impact of their colleague's absence by continuing to provide students with quality instruction and feedback on their performance. Their willingness to go above and beyond has earned them this recognition. This Super Pat goes to _____ .*

The Super Pat award would be handed out to the teachers amid great applause, and Dan would move on to celebrate the next story of effort and achievement special and unique to our school culture and our teacher teams. Dan taught all of us how to use celebration as a tool to build community. He was an insightful leader who used celebration to connect us to our shared purpose and to create a sense of belonging among the faculty, staff, and students.

What were the behind-the-scenes planning elements that made these public celebrations so successful?

1. **Effective identification.** Two months before the celebration event, the administrative team, faculty, and staff would submit names of individuals and teams worthy of a Super Pat. The leadership team would review the recommendations and make the final decisions.

2. **Effective criteria.** Any "above and beyond" adult actions that moved the school closer to its vision and values in any of the Five E categories of the vision were eligible for celebration.

3. **Effective rewards.** Awardees received a variety of Super Pat rewards ranging from a paperweight, to bookends, to a book that might reflect their hobby or interest. Individual teachers as well as teacher teams were recognized. The story that was read about each winner was recorded in writing and the written story shared as part of the reward.

4. **Effective storytelling.** Connecting the story to student success, describing the predicament that was solved, highlighting the details

and effects of the adult actions, and saving the name(s) of the awardees to the end of the announcement were important elements of the
process to build excitement.

Kouzes and Posner capture the essence of this critical storytelling aspect of
school leadership, quoting Harvard Professor Howard Gardner:

> The artful creation and articulation of stories constitutes a funda-
> mental part of the leader's vocation. Stories speak to both parts
> of the human mind—its reason and emotion. And I suggest, fur-
> ther, that it is stories of identity—narratives that help individuals
> think about and feel who they are, where they come from, and
> where they are headed—that constitute the single most powerful
> weapon in the leader's literary arsenal. (Gardner, as cited in Kouzes
> & Posner, 1999, p. 105)

A tradition at Stevenson since 1992, and presented to faculty and staff twice
a year—at midyear and at the end of the school year in June—more than eight
hundred Super Pats have been received over the years, and every one of them
represents a compelling story crucial to leading our school organization *forward*—
into the next cycle of results and actions that lead into our future.

By celebrating your history, you model examples for others to follow in future
cycles of growth and improvement. Tall poppies allowed!

# Study Guide ■ ■ ■ ■ ■

Visit **go.solution-tree.com/plcbooks** to download this study guide and the worksheets mentioned in it.

## *Examining My Leadership Perspective*

1. Experienced PLC leaders know they must monitor the "right thing" adult actions described in the vision and values, and eventually become tight about them. What is in your personal list of right things? Why are these items on your list?

2. Have you had a watershed PLC leadership moment that fits the loose-tight model? What was a vision component that you personally cared so much about that moved you to respond? In what ways did your response show that you were becoming a drift-resistant leader?

3. How do you define autonomy and defend boundaries for the teams you lead? How do you help those you lead to understand the difference between autonomy and independence? To visualize this idea, refer to figure 2.1, Adult Behaviors Within the Vision and Values Boundary Box (page 47).

4. What is your leadership plan to communicate at the tier 3 vertical level in a way that is efficient and relationally effective? How do you plan to respond to selected non-negotiable vision points to keep monitored vital behaviors to a manageable number? How do you plan to respond with immediate and corrective feedback to the work products of the team? You may find it helpful to complete the worksheet *Moving Vision Into Action*.

5. Think back to the definition of the discipline of accountability and celebration (page 36). How do you interpret the expression *with consequences* in terms of how you make decisions and how you communicate those decisions to your teams?

6. Examine the current accountability and celebration system used in your school or area of school leadership. How would you describe its effectiveness? What are its strengths and its weaknesses? What would you do to improve the current system in order to improve actions for sustained change?

## *Extending My Leadership Perspective*

1. Think about the attributes of the terms *accountability* and *celebration* (see table 2.1, page 37). As a team, take time to define these terms.

Write one-word emotions and feelings that generally surface with each word. What do the responses reveal about individual perceptions of accountability and celebration? How can you use these responses to bring greater clarity, understanding, and appreciation of what accountability and celebration actually mean within your area of school leadership? Use the *Accountability-Celebration Matrix* worksheet for this activity.

2. What was your initial reaction when you read about the three tiers of accountability—self, lateral, and vertical? In what ways did this information lead you to examine the distribution of accountability within your areas of leadership?

3. Using your best judgment, for every teacher team or administrative team in your sphere of influence, identify the most commonly used tier of accountability: *self*-accountability, *lateral* accountability, or *vertical* accountability. Then match each team to the appropriate tier for an identified *vital behavior* for the current school year. Use the *Tiers of Accountability and Celebration to Vision Action* worksheet for this activity. (Alternatively, ask each team to self-identify its tier placement.) Then reflect and respond to the following questions.

   - Tier 1 teachers or teacher teams: How can you use their model to influence the behavior of others?

   - Tier 2 teachers or teacher teams: How can you better harness peer pressure and support for coherent implementation of the vital behavior at the team level?

   - Tier 3 teachers or teacher teams: What types of structural support should you provide to help each teacher or teacher team to move into tier 1 or tier 2 self-directed behavior for the vital and tight vision action or behavior?

4. What can you do over the next few months to target two or three teams and help them work together to build greater lateral accountability within the social system of the PLC?

5. How can you begin to use district benchmark tests as well as other forms of team-level assessments to support the Stage 5 work of your teams and make the cycle of continuous improvement occur more than once a year or semester?

   - How will you provide immediate and corrective feedback to the team on its use of the results?

- How will you provide the time for the team to craft the required formative assessment response to the benchmark data and use that response to shape instruction?

- How will you create a culture of candor and transparency in the team discussions around the results?

- How will you ensure all teachers share the results with students and require all students use their errors to demonstrate learning based on those mistakes?

6. Revisit figure 2.3, The Accountability and Celebration Model for Continuous Improvement (page 60). How can you use the model to help team members better understand the role they play in sustaining effective implementation of the vision on an ongoing, day-to-day basis?

CHAPTER 3

*The Discipline of*

# Service and Sharing

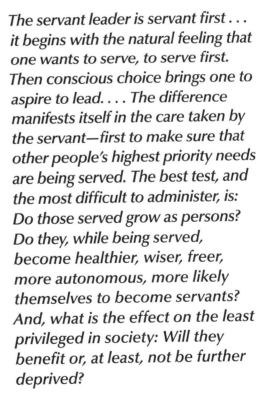

*The servant leader is servant first . . . it begins with the natural feeling that one wants to serve, to serve first. Then conscious choice brings one to aspire to lead. . . . The difference manifests itself in the care taken by the servant—first to make sure that other people's highest priority needs are being served. The best test, and the most difficult to administer, is: Do those served grow as persons? Do they, while being served, become healthier, wiser, freer, more autonomous, more likely themselves to become servants? And, what is the effect on the least privileged in society: Will they benefit or, at least, not be further deprived?*

—Robert Greenleaf

PLC leadership is as much about investing time and energy in your own growth as in the growth of those in your sphere of influence. In your leadership role, you foster a culture in which all individuals (yourself included), working in highly collaborative teams, grow in their ability to make effective contributions to the well-being of the school. A distinctive aspect of effective PLC leaders is that they are adept at adult capacity development—among all adults in their sphere of influence, continuously.

The theme of this chapter is creating a relationally intelligent school culture in which the cycle of continuous improvement is seamlessly maintained. Such a culture is one in which individuals accept responsibility for their actions; they hold themselves accountable, and they become aware of others in the social sphere of the professional learning community.

PLC leaders foster the development of individual and collective craft knowledge regarding improved student learning experiences by creating a service and relational culture in their area of school leadership. A service and sharing culture requires adults willing to be accountable to the shared vision as well as to the impact of their words and actions on others. Let's review the definition of the discipline of service and sharing:

**The leadership work of demonstrating personal accountability to the shared vision and to all who may be affected by your thoughts, words, actions, and inactions**

In the context of this definition, you have a responsibility to build shared knowledge about and relational capacity toward the shared vision. This requires you to notice others, to serve others, and to demonstrate, as needed, acceptance or tough empathy toward others. In brief, your role is to develop a culture of sharing that builds peer knowledge and relational capacity among all you lead and influence. This requires you to build your own emotional intelligence and your own knowledge so you can serve and share effectively with others. This leadership discipline is not an event, but rather an ongoing process for creating greater relational capacity for every faculty and staff member, no matter how strong or how weak he or she is in any aspect of the profession. This discipline provides the frame for one of the most critical pursuits of professional learning community leadership: *the improvement of everyone's knowledge capacity through ongoing professional development.*

As a school leader, I had learned the importance of extending my own knowledge. I knew I needed to stay current with "leading edge" information that provided the *technical* resources of my craft. I had developed the habit of reading everything I could in my specific areas of school leadership, and then connecting it into my work at Stevenson. In 1998, I was introduced to two books. The first was *On Becoming a Servant Leader* (Frick & Spears, 1996), an anthology of the writings of Robert K. Greenleaf. The second book was *Stewardship: Choosing Service Over Self-Interest* (1993) by Peter Block. In my microscopic world of mathematics and science leadership, these thought leaders were new to me. Greenleaf was best known for his essays on servant leadership. Block was well known for his work on empowerment and relationship building in the workplace. Block (1993) defines *stewardship* in the institutional setting as "attending to the service brought to each employee, customer and community. To be accountable to those we have power over" (p. 22). Block quotes Greenleaf: "The first order of business is to build a group of people who, under the influence of the institution, grow taller, and become healthier, stronger, more autonomous" (p. 22). In other words: tall poppies allowed. Autonomy allowed. Servant leadership allowed. *Accountability to the vision and values and to the growth of others toward the vision and values required*—including, as a member of a PLC teacher team, an expanded accountability to those students you do not directly teach.

These two thought leaders had a profound impact on my understanding of school leadership from a relational skill and knowledge capacity development perspective. Becoming familiar with their thinking about leadership enabled me to change my view of the primary pursuit of professional learning communities. Consequently, my new focus became building the *individual and collective* capacity of all adults toward full engagement in, and commitment to, the vital behaviors that improve student achievement. I realized the most effective means to attain that focus was through development of a culture of service and sharing throughout the school.

Judith Sowder (2007) points out that teachers working together in teams to develop professionally "create, expand, and exchange knowledge about their practice" (p. 186). In turn, such activity leads to a subsequent change in actual classroom practice. The caveat here is that professional development and learning needs to be an ongoing and sustainable activity embedded in practice. Support for this caveat comes from Linda Darling-Hammond and Nikole Richardson (2009), who state "professional development lasting 14 or fewer hours showed *no effect* on [teacher] learning. The largest effects were for programs offering 30–100 hours spread out over 6–12 months" (p. 49). The ongoing sharing of knowledge that characterizes the PLC culture exemplifies these researchers' observations.

In forming professional learning communities, the initial effort is often directed at creating a culture of collaboration. Fullan cites researcher Nancy Dixon, who studied knowledge sharing and suggests the evidence supports taking a more indirect approach: "If people begin sharing ideas about issues they see as really important, then sharing itself creates a learning culture" (Dixon, as quoted in Fullan, 2001, p. 84). Dixon calls attention to the important qualifier: if people begin sharing ideas *about issues they see as really important*," then effective collaboration is likely to result.

Although your leadership must focus on results, PLC leadership is also about the tenacious pursuit of a culture of service and sharing that will significantly impact those results. Being a school leader bears a moral responsibility to become someone who makes a significant and positive impact on the knowledge development of others—to help others reach their full potential. PLC leaders are stewards of adult learning. The tension that lies within this leadership discipline is that it is highly relational, intimate, and dependent on those being influenced to be successful. In this context, you have less control. This discipline draws on the art of leadership as much as the skill. It is about how well you personally lead and relate to others in order to turn the vision into action.

Growth in the discipline of service and sharing will require a lot of training in personal development. It requires you to take responsibility to think, act, and speak in a way that makes *you* accountable to all those you lead and influence. It turns everything upside down. Yes, you are the leader. You have positional authority and influence. You are the last line of defense for accountability and celebration. Your role is to make sure others *act* on their knowledge of mutually accepted actions for best practice. And yet, you are also accountable to others— what a paradox. In fact, the more effectively you lead in the discipline of service and sharing, the less you will be needed by those within your sphere of influence, and the more likely they will become servant leaders themselves.

Strength in the discipline of service and sharing means you are more concerned about the welfare of others and the welfare of the school and programs you lead than anything else. It means you understand that this discipline requires you to pursue a better relational version of yourself, forever.

# Growing Emotional Intelligence

Disciplined PLC leaders build *relationally* with others. This pursuit is much easier for some PLC leaders than it is for others. Trying hard to be more relational just doesn't come naturally to some of us. Over the years, I have known many faculty members who wanted to be team leaders, grade-level leaders, district coordinators, academic coaches, or assistant principals. Sometimes, although these individuals were fairly well skilled at the vision discipline, they were not yet strong enough relationally with other adults. I knew that if I allowed them to be placed immediately into an expanded leadership position, problems would arise for those in their leadership sphere of influence. They first had to make a personal commitment to work on improving their emotional intelligence.

According to Daniel Goleman and his colleagues (2002), emotionally intelligent leaders give praise, create a positive climate, criticize constructively, provide direction, support people's needs, and "frame the group's mission in ways that give more meaning to each person's contribution—or not. All these acts help determine a leader's primal emotional impact" (p. 9). Furthermore, the authors indicate that emotional climate drives performance results, the leader drives the emotional climate of the workplace, and the leader's emotional intelligence drives how people feel and perform: "How well leaders manage their moods and effect everyone else's moods, then, becomes not just a private matter but a factor in how well a business will do" (p. 18). The more demanding and stressful the situation— such as working in chronically low-performing schools, working in a district with severe budget cutbacks, dealing with the elimination of viable and necessary support programs, and coping with public scrutiny—the more essential it is for the school leaders to have a well-developed emotional intelligence.

To further highlight the critical importance of the leaders' ability to serve and share, Pfeffer and Sutton (2006) in *Hard Facts, Dangerous Half-Truths, and Total Nonsense* report there is evidence that "poor relational leaders will drive skilled and motivated workers out of the profession, or even worse, cause them to withhold discretionary effort" (p. 191). Furthermore, they report that researchers find "60%–75% of employees in any organization report that the worst or most stressful aspect of their job is their immediate supervisor" (p. 191). The idea that those you lead and influence are holding back effort, and that as their immediate supervisor you could be the reason, is a bit daunting and unnerving.

I have several colleagues, some with whom I worked at Stevenson, who claim you cannot get better at this leadership discipline. Either you have the ability to relate well, or you don't. If you have relationally sharp elbows at thirty, you'll still have them at forty. Either a commitment to care about the growth of others resides within you, or it doesn't. "Go ahead," they say, "act on the suggestions for this leadership discipline, but it won't matter."

I strongly disagree. So does Goleman (2001) in *The Emotionally Intelligent Workplace.* In his framework for emotional intelligence, Goleman identifies personal competencies for improvement including empathy, service orientation, developing others, conflict management, teamwork, and collaboration. Development of these competencies begins with the PLC leader as a model, and that leader's influence subsequently serves to build these competencies in others. Which of these emotional intelligence competencies are in your leadership repertoire?

It seems the "art" aspect of the discipline of service and sharing lies in developing the innate emotional intelligence deep within you. To be an administrator means to administer or "care for." You must care for those you lead, but not without accountability to substance and purpose. Doug Reeves (2006) describes this tension:

> Surely there is a middle ground between leadership by Barney the Dinosaur and leadership by Attila the Hun. Relational leadership does not depend on false affirmations provided in vain attempts to build the self-esteem of subordinates, but rather on the trust and integrity that are the foundation of any enduring relationship. (p. 39)

Kouzes and Posner (2006) highlight the importance of strong service-oriented relationships in a surprising analysis from their own leadership studies:

> Longitudinal studies of corporate executives reveal that the single best predictor of career success is the relationship they had with their very first supervisor. The character and quality of that relationship—for example, the expectations that your first supervisor had about your work potential—are more important than where you went to school, what grades you got, what you studied, who your parents were, what field or industry you were in, and the like. (p. 34)

The success of future faculty, staff, and colleagues is predicated on their relationship with *you* and the emotional climate you create and support in your area of school leadership. That brings deeper meaning to your responsibility to serve others well. And it will take intentional training to grow in this leadership discipline. Through direct effort alone, you may not become as strong relationally as you need to be. By becoming a relationally disciplined leader, you will move beyond the fluctuations between good and not-so-good relational days.

Reeves (2006) provides insight into how to become a relationally stronger leader. Our leadership team at Stevenson used his insight to develop our relational skills and awareness with one another. His four practices for improving relational intelligence (pp. 40–42) follow, accompanied by commentaries that our leadership team generated:

1. **"Listen without interrupting."** Record your next leadership team or teacher team meeting. How often do your team members interrupt one another? How could your team members better listen to one another?

2. **"Practice empathy through deliberate inquiry."** How often do your leadership team or teacher team members seek first to understand the meaning and intent of the words of others? How often do you hear, "Tell me more" or "How could I support you in this work?" in your daily conversations?

3. **"Never betray a private conversation."** Is the fine line between what is for public knowledge and what is for private knowledge crystal clear for your leadership or teacher team? As teams pursue greater transparency, how well does everyone respect the confidences of private conversations—including those conversations of the team?

4. **"Exhibit genuine passion for the people you serve."** How well do members of your leadership team exhibit genuine interest and pay private and personal attention to the individuals in their sphere of influence?

You can get better relationally. These four practices provide a great basis for measuring how you and those on your team(s) are doing. You *can* become a more intimate leader and relate better to others. It really is a matter of conscious choice. And then you must ask, exactly who are those others that I am to involve in service and sharing?

# Cultivating an N-S-E-W Sphere of Influence

You can choose to lead *north* to those who have positional authority over you, *south* to those entrusted to your leadership, or *east* or *west* to those who are your lateral peers. School leaders often hear the familiar "caught in the middle" complaint from principals, assistant principals, curriculum directors, coaches, department chairs, and grade-level leaders. This complaint provides justification to abdicate responsibility for their work, they think, because they have no "real" authority. Recently a middle school department leader said to me, "What do you want me to do? The principal won't back me up on this!"

My response was simple: "I want you to lead in every direction—especially those to your north. I want you to relate with and positively impact your principal—to influence his or her thinking and to build into his or her knowledge capacity. It is why we are a learning community."

At times, everyone feels caught in the middle, including the superintendent. And the way to fight through that feeling is to serve in all four directions—to become an N-S-E-W leader.

Imagine your sphere of service—your sphere of responsibility to think, speak, and act as if you are personally accountable to all who may be affected by your thoughts, words, actions, and inactions—as a four-direction *value-added* responsibility. Figure 3.1 provides a visual representation of this expanded understanding of your leadership influence.

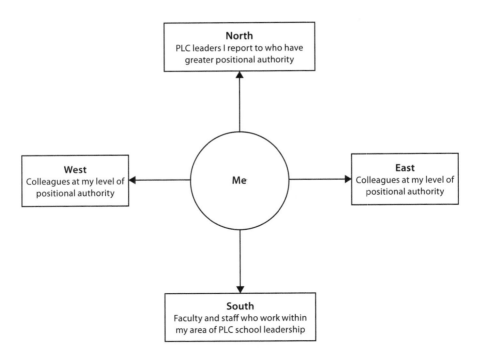

**Figure 3.1: The N-S-E-W PLC sphere of influence chart.**

*Visit go.solution-tree.com/plcbooks to download a reproducible version of this figure.*

A distinctive difference between PLC leaders and non-PLC leaders is their willingness to understand the nature of their relational impact on those to their north. Successful PLC leaders take the time to inform leaders to their north, add to the strengths of those leaders, and introduce those leaders to good leadership resources. In your area of influence, you can provide the leaders to your north with the research and resources necessary to inform collective decision making. By developing positive relationships with those to your north, you provide service that overcomes potential relational barriers.

Have you possibly encountered leaders who lack clear direction, who are selfish, who quickly change direction, who vacillate, or who seem generally ineffective? Yes, they exist! Yet you, as a PLC leader, must not lean away from such individuals. You must tenaciously lean *toward* them, publicly affirming authentic strengths and privately working to support weaknesses. Gossiping, complaining, and dramatizing are *not* the way of the PLC leader or, for that matter, any of the adults in a professional learning community. PLC leaders have no tolerance for these relational toxins.

Another distinction between PLC school leaders and non-PLC school leaders is the willingness to pursue lateral accountability and celebration of their peers. PLC leaders and teachers embrace the notion of E-W discussions with and influence on one another. One of the great benefits of effective E-W service and sharing is the way it eventually will lighten team members' workloads. To add value to those on your team, you provide solutions to problems, not just point out the problems. You serve the team by performing tasks that are not necessarily your "job," and no matter the circumstances, you do not make excuses—in particular, you avoid blaming those to your north.

Looking back on those early days of PLC development, I remember being surprised that our faculty and staff just did not naturally seem to get along with one another at times. I honestly thought that if I focused their effort on meaningful work and tasks, they would naturally want to do them together and treat each other with dignity and grace. It did not occur to me that we needed a professional development plan for how to relate with one another more effectively and how to deeply *listen* to one another. We needed norms for how to behave together. We needed to learn how to disagree yet still respect one another. We might think that as a profession, teaching draws adults who are highly relational. What I discovered was that although certain adults were highly relational with students, they often lacked the skills to be open and vulnerable with one another. For some of our faculty and administrators, transparency with colleagues (even if for the greater good of student learning and achievement) was a symbol of weakness—of not being able to do the job independently. And pre-PLC, our teachers and leaders did not view it as their responsibility to influence those in their E-W sphere and become more transparent with one another.

What words and actions of yours impact those in your north, south, east, and west spheres of influence? Are you willing to "lead up" to those with positional authority above you? Are you willing to lead across to your colleagues and peers? Are you willing to lead south in such a way that it empowers those entrusted to your leadership? Does your willingness to lead south empower those individuals, in turn, to lead north—to influence and share with you? Does your modeling enable them to lead east and west (to influence their colleagues and peers, to exercise tier 2 accountability), and lead themselves (tier 1 accountability)? Moreover, as Robert Greenleaf so eloquently asked in the opening epigraph of this chapter, will those served by the leaders [you and the teachers] have an effect on the "least privileged in society [many of your students]: Will [the students] benefit or, at least, not be further deprived?" (Frick & Spears, 1996, p. 2)

As your professional learning community matures, more adults will pursue the responsibility of N-S-E-W communications, and as a result, issues of relational immaturity will begin to dissipate. More importantly, as you develop skill in the discipline of service and sharing, those in your south will spend more time leading one another laterally toward the right things of the vision. Consequently, they will need less monitoring from you as a leader to their north. Reciprocal relationships will abound, and lateral accountability of service among team members will eventually blossom.

# Pursuing Level 5 Leadership

The chain of service and sharing looks like this: you work hard to continuously improve and develop your knowledge and your ability to lead relationally with others. By making a better person out of yourself, you become someone that a faculty member, staff member, or administrative colleague would *choose* to understand, or be persuaded, motivated, inspired, or influenced by. As you lead teachers and they in turn lead you, they do the same for their students. Leading and following become simultaneous events, reciprocal, and collaborative.

Servant leadership is a paradox. You lead by serving others. You need to be humble, yet strong-willed for the greater good. Collins (2001), in his book *Good to Great: Why Some Companies Make the Leap . . . and Others Don't*, offers empirical research regarding the type of leadership qualities necessary to achieve great outcomes. In your case as a PLC leader, great outcomes mean improvement in both student learning and development. Collins's research parallels many of the relational pursuits of a PLC leader, and his chapter on "Level 5 leadership" describes specific qualities of the most effective, or "Level 5," leaders. These qualities include personal humility combined with professional will for the school, a compelling modesty, fanatical drive to produce sustained great results, a workmanlike diligence, and the ability to take full responsibility (self-accountability) for disappointing results.

In 2005, Collins released *Good to Great and the Social Sectors*, partly in response to numerous requests from schools, government, and other nonprofit organizations seeking information about effective leadership. Could *Good to Great* apply to the social sector, and if so, how do Level 5 leaders get things done within a more diffused power structure base? Collins (2005) points out, appropriately, that one of the major challenges facing social sector leaders lies in the more legislative type of leadership common to the social sector: "legislative leadership relies more upon persuasion and shared interests to create the conditions for the right decisions to happen" (p. 11).

The Level 5 leadership qualities that emerged from Collins's research provide an excellent measure for progress along the *discipline of service and sharing* continuum. Compare Level 5 leadership to what Collins (2005) describes as Level 4 leadership: "the effective leader catalyzes commitment to and vigorous pursuit of a clear and compelling vision, stimulating higher performance standards" (p. 11).

Level 4 leadership is actually very good, but ultimately, it's not sufficient for sustainability. Imagine a room full of Level 4 leaders in your school, pushing on the school improvement wheel. A "vigorous pursuit of a compelling vision" and "higher performance standards" would be the norm. Now imagine those Level 4 leaders are gone, having retired or moved up and on to a new and different leadership position in another school or district. Imagine Level 4 teachers and administrators who are transferred or lost due to reduction in force, and key staff members, parents, or community and board members who leave the district due to job changes. What happens to the school or district when the Level 4 leaders leave? Entropy, backsliding, and chaos set in. The life cycle of an effective school is short: it typically takes just a decade to become great and then fall. As Jonathan Saphier (2005) observes, "In every case I know, what rose and fell was not the curriculum, the safety of the neighborhood, or the sources at the school's disposal. It was the leadership among the adults in the school" (p. 111). Unfortunately, Level 4 leadership doesn't ensure longevity of sustained change.

Great, enduring, and sustainable schools and school districts are populated with enough Level 5 leaders that the PLC culture and the pursuit for great outputs of student and adult performance endure even after the Level 5 leaders are no longer present. Level 5 leaders possess a compelling personal modesty ("This great school is *not* about me") with a fearless professional will for the good of the school, district, or program of school leadership. A great school is about *others*—the faculty, staff, students, and parents. Collins (2001) describes this paradox as the duality between "personal humility and professional will" (p. 22). Not surprisingly, this characteristic applies to the best type of PLC leaders: those who lead by serving the growth and development of others toward the vision and values of the school.

Like all aspects of professional learning communities, leadership is complex. There is no magic five-step process to becoming a Level 5 professional learning community leader. Leaders who possess Level 5 attributes pursue a balance between humility and strong will.

## Showing Humility

Professional learning community cultures do not have much tolerance for egotistical leaders. Collins (2001) indicates that Level 5 leaders are not "first and foremost about what they *get*—fame, fortune, adulation, power, whatever." Rather, leaders can evolve into Level 5 if they are about "what they *build*, create, and contribute" (p. 36, emphasis added). This is true for you, and it is true for everyone in your sphere of influence. Teacher teams will only be as effective as their collective ability to *build something great*.

Can you see the beauty of school leadership that is simultaneously humble and strong-willed? Humility of self combined with strong will for the school? What a wonderful paradox. Personal humility is not timidity. It is *not* a lack of aggressiveness or an attempt to convince others you are incompetent or undeserving of praise. Circumspection, modesty, willingness to give credit where and when it is due, and the ability to provide constructive criticism are attributes of a leader who knows how to serve and share. There is a way to be "tough as nails" that signals to others your "tightness" on an issue is not about you—in fact, it may not even be about them—but rather about what it takes to make the school become a great place for learning. Professional will is an expression of your *tolerance level* for actions or inactions of others toward the shared vision and values.

There is a temptation to look at the N-S-E-W influence model and say, "All right! I'm in the middle! It's all about me, the leader!" Actually, that's ego speak. Dee Hock (2000) makes the point that 50 percent of our time should be spent on self-leadership, and we should spend the other 50 percent on the leadership of others. Part of that "self" work is to figure out your own way to attaining humility. For me, as I learned to serve better those in my N-S-E-W sphere, I began the gradual pursuit of focusing less on myself and more on others; less on having all the answers and more on listening for answers from others; less on taking credit for success and more on giving credit for success to others; more on taking responsibility when things weren't going well and less on blaming others.

From a PLC perspective, humility is acknowledging that no individual adult will ever have all the answers and that effective teaching and learning *require* the pursuit of continuous improvement and growth. Resting on our current understanding of "what works" is prideful folly. If anything, PLC leaders embrace an appropriate sense of current reality, serve *together* to improve on that reality, and celebrate the accomplishments of others without concern for who has the solutions. They ensure others get the credit they deserve and accept that as leaders, they won't always know the answers.

In the fall of 1990, four years into my journey as a school leader, we were in a team meeting. One of my administrative colleagues asked the principal how we should best respond to specific student issues within our EL program. I had become accustomed to his responses being typically succinct and clear-focused, with high standards for immediate implementation. But this time, it was different. His response was simply "I don't know." He did go on to identify other avenues of inquiry and follow-up, such as national recommendations, additional local school actions in the area and their potential successful responses, and so on. But I heard none of that conversation. All I remember thinking was that he said "I don't know" in front of all of us. It was as if a burden had been lifted from my shoulders.

His model gave me permission to say "I don't know" with my own staff. It gave me the freedom not to need all the answers (a pride issue on my part really), and eventually, it opened me up to becoming a more inquiry-based leader. In turn, my action empowered my own staff to take more responsibility for their growth and improvement and rely less on me. My communication became more "talking with" others and less "talking to" others.

# Building an Expanded Leadership Base

Developing leadership capacity of interdependent work groups or teams further enhances the development of individual leadership capacity among all of the adults. In 1998, Wilfred Drath discussed this new idea of group leadership:

> The focus of leadership development activity shifts away from the individual and toward the interdependent work group. In the future, leadership development will be aimed at improvements in the quality of interrelating among people engaged in interdependent work. This brings leadership development into the domain of what we have come to think of as team development (team building) or even organization development. The new idea of leadership invites a different conception of the team and the organization: not as an entity outside the individual that the individual "joins," but rather the sum total of all interactions. (p. 422)

Drath's description implies the need to expand the leadership base in the school or district beyond the actions of a single leader. PLC leadership is about becoming part of a distributed process shared by many. Leaders who develop collaborative strategies for the purpose of building adult knowledge capacity are committed to a central pursuit of a professional learning community. The more teachers become aware of their power to drive change—change around the *right set of collective values*—the more likely they are to take ownership of their work. And there is a greater level of certainty that the collaborative strategies will be successful when built around research that leads to improved student achievement.

In a sense, the PLC leader, as a servant leader, becomes the steward of the professional learning community and its values. You ensure the shared values are protected. In a PLC, the role of the teacher extends beyond the classroom to embrace new collaborative structures. Similarly, the role of school leader extends beyond the office of the principal, department chair, or curriculum specialist. School leadership becomes a much more complex process in a collaborative environment. *In a learning community, every teacher is expected to exercise leadership.* East-west influence abounds. Lateral accountability abounds.

Collaborative teacher team work must be built around the N-S-E-W leadership paradigm of what is best for adults and *students*. Students also want meaningful teaching and learning experiences. Pedro Noguera (2004) cites a Harvard University survey in which students reported they wanted a more interactive teaching style, a more relevant curriculum, and school rules responsive to their living circumstances, and to have a voice in their education. Just as administrative leaders must engage faculty in collaborative dialogue, so must teachers, as leaders, seek students' input and engage them in their own educational process. Facilitating student-engaged learning is part of the real work of all teacher teams.

PLC leadership culture encourages all stakeholders to act as one community of responsibility. PLC leadership is based on a different kind of authority, an authority embedded in the vision to which individuals hold themselves accountable—responding from within, to become self-managing and self-aware. This is the self-accountability tier described in chapter 2 (page 56). Instead of following the leader (the *who*), the emphasis is on following the commitments, promises, obligations, validated research, sound principles, or agreed-upon standards—the vision and values of the school (the *what*). Resisting the tendency to accept mediocre performance is one of the intentions of a professional learning community. As Sergiovanni (2005) suggests, "In communities of responsibility, it is norms, values, beliefs, purposes, goals, standards, hopes and dreams that provide the ideas for leadership" (p. 142). This is what it means to become a professional learning community of adults, regardless of each individual's N-S-E-W position, role, or title.

School systems measure their outputs not in terms of profit but rather in terms of student success (improved achievement and improved social-emotional growth). Collins (2005) clarifies:

> A great organization is one that delivers superior performance and makes a distinctive impact over a long period of time. For a business, financial returns are a perfectly legitimate measure of performance. For a social sector organization, however, performance must be assessed relative to mission, not financial returns. In the social sectors the critical question is not "How much money do we make per dollar of invested capital?" but "How effectively do we deliver on our mission and make a distinctive impact?" (p. 5)

This distinction of outputs in the social sector merges well with the model of continuous improvement through adult and student actions that take responsibility to improve student learning and achievement goals. Drath (2008) also thinks about leadership by "framing it in terms of outcomes: Leadership is about producing agreement on *direction*, a framework for *alignment* and a sense of *commitment* to the collective work" (p. 21, emphasis in the original). In his framework (which Drath calls DAC—direction, alignment, and commitment), leadership is as much about the pursuit and commitment to vision outcomes as it is about the people who need to get it done.

PLC leadership exists in the center of these two leadership paradigms. On one hand, Collins's work indicates PLC leaders should *serve* others to engage in the work of DAC, and on the other hand, Drath's work indicates PLC leaders should *ensure* that DAC happens as a way to serve others.

For me, becoming a servant leader was a much harder task that required discipline, intentional training, and practice. I did not naturally think of others first. That didn't mean I wasn't a good leader, but after twelve years of working and teaching alone, and becoming a very self-directed learner, it did not come naturally for me to seek answers and to learn from others. I thought I was supposed to do that for them; after all, isn't that why they needed me as their leader? I had to learn how to become a better servant leader.

# Creating a Relational Culture

An original intent of building PLC cultures in schools was the pursuit of improved student achievement through collaborative teacher decisions on what students need to know and learn, how best to assess that expected knowledge, and how to provide a coherent and timely response when students don't learn. This pursuit is best achieved when administrators, faculty, and staff are more empowered and responsible.

This focus on student learning led to a significant shift in the role of school leaders. Their leadership role became to foster collegial participation by relinquishing control of the team to the teacher members. In a PLC, the leader takes on a role that is more legislative and consequently more difficult to fulfill. Providing direction and knowledge while at the same time providing empowerment and space presents new challenges for many school leaders—and calls for training in the discipline of service and sharing.

Leaders can implement a number of training practices to develop their proficiency in this discipline. There are ten practices I have found effective in my relational growth and development activities as a school leader:

1. Share (or don't share) your thoughts

2. Exercise good judgment

3. Use good judgment criteria

4. Be "interruptible"

5. Establish personal intimacy

6. Build communities of practice

7. Build the relational capacity of the team

8. Measure and teach the softer side of team sharing

9. Choose to be an inequity eraser

10. Accept others

## *Share (or Don't Share) Your Thoughts*

During the early years of our growth as an administrative team at Stevenson, we had quite a few sharing moments that were dysfunctional, that lacked service orientation. Certain administrators (like me) loved to talk and dominate the discussion items on the agenda. Dominators tend to be confident and like to quickly pepper everyone with their thoughts. Such "helpful" observations can easily cross the line into ego: "Listen to the sound of my voice, don't I sound great? Aren't I a wonderful contributor to our team?" Pride alert! Four or five leaders on our team were like that. And did we ever jockey for position and opportunity to share our words for the good of the cause! The truth is, we could have served the leadership team better if some of us would have remained silent from time to time, or asked questions that would have invited (and allowed) the participation of others. We needed to be accountable for the nature of our participation in the meetings.

The other source of dysfunction came from those leaders who tended toward inaction: being too quiet or refusing to share their thoughts and words. These kinds of individuals are also accountable for their behavior. Individuals who are too silent, too restricted with words, or too reserved contribute to two problems in a group. First, their behavior can engender suspicion, even fear, among those they lead: "What is she really thinking? Why is she so silent?" If people don't know someone's thinking or position on an issue, they may feel that the person lacks openness and transparency and perhaps shouldn't be trusted. Second, the lack of participation causes a void in conversation and discussion that the dominators are only too happy to fill. Consequently, the shared wisdom of the team becomes limited to the shared wisdom of the few. Neither type of individual is a role model of effective leadership behavior. Neither type contributes to the success of the team. But what's the solution for such dysfunctional behavior?

Toothpicks. Our leadership team solved the problem by using toothpicks. At each team meeting, each person received three toothpicks. When you spoke, you placed your toothpick in the center of the table. When you were out of toothpicks, you were done speaking for the meeting. Conversation was carefully measured, and by the end of the meeting, the silent types were the only ones left who could talk. Eventually we moved to "raise your hand," waiting to be called on by the team leader, often using round-robin or "first word–last word" techniques for more distributed sharing.

Being crystal clear about who is driving the meeting agenda and making sure that time is not wasted are factors critical to the success of a team meeting. Do you or your colleagues need to serve the team by using a more accountable process of sharing? Take a close look, and monitor your communication patterns. You serve others through a genuine intent to speak *and* to listen. Your ability to listen and participate well signals the importance you place on the conversation of the team as well as respect for individuals on the team.

## *Exercise Good Judgment*

What is the last really difficult decision you needed to make in your area of school leadership? How did it go? In making that decision, did you exercise good judgment and serve the needs of the adults and students in your sphere of influence?

Personal accountability to those affected by your thoughts, words, and actions requires you to consistently demonstrate good judgment. Leadership authorities Noel Tichy and Warren Bennis (2007) suggest in their book *Judgment: How Winning Leaders Make Great Calls* that with good judgment, little else matters. Without it, nothing else matters. They state:

> Leadership is, at its marrow, the chronicle of judgment calls; this is the leader's biography. Good leadership requires good judgment. Long-term success is the sole marker of good judgment. It's not "The operation was a success, but the patient died." It's not "He acted brilliantly, but the outcome was poor." Judgment is successful only when the outcome achieves the espoused goals of the institution. Period. Enthusiasm, good intentions, and hard work may help, but without good results, they don't count. (p. 5)

Again, results come to the surface. Our leadership decisions and judgment calls, once executed and acted upon, need to demonstrate student improvement. Ultimately, your decisions and the judgments on which they are based will be determined to be good or bad depending on the results of the actions. The goal is to build the capacity of all those adults in your N-S-E-W sphere of influence also to make good judgment calls, calls consistent with the vision and values of the school. You serve by creating a culture that understands how to make good judgments.

Not surprisingly, serving by exercising good judgment begins with the way in which you enhance your ability to sense when there is a need for a judgment call, and then making the call. Your self-knowledge comes into play. Tichy and Bennis

(2007) provide further insight into how a good leader uses self-knowledge *and the knowledge of others* to make good judgments:

> The quality of a person's judgment depends to a large degree on his or her ability to marshal resources and to interact well with the appropriate constituencies. . . . Do you know who you are? Do you have clear values about what you are trying to accomplish? Do you have clear values about what you will and will not do to achieve your goals? Do you know what you know and what you don't know? Can you empathize with others and anticipate their possible responses? Can you draw on your own experiences for future guidance? Are you willing to learn? Leaders who exercise good judgment calls are able to listen, reframe their thinking, and give up old paradigms . . . you are always looking for ways of doing it better. (p. 40)

Forward-thinking PLC leaders are not only willing to give up on old paradigms; they are also willing to seek out, create, and respond to new paradigms for the best way to enhance student learning. These shifts often can occur in the wake of learning from a bad judgment call. Have you ever made a judgment call that led to a lousy decision? Things didn't work out too well? Could have been handled better? Of course you have. Every PLC leader has exercised poor judgment occasionally. It happens. The goal is to not let poor judgment happen very often. Think of your example of poor judgment. It is filled with lessons on how to make better judgment calls, better decisions in the future. And if anyone was harmed as a result of that judgment call, it is you who must ante up and be the first to apologize.

## Use Good Judgment Criteria

In 1987, my second year as a school leader, I decided that the faculty in my leadership area (math and science) were not sufficiently sharing the workload. I made the judgment call that all teachers should move from two preparations (or courses to teach) to three preparations for the following year. This judgment was based on my previous personal experience; before I became a school leader, I had always taught at least three different types of courses. It was also based on my thoughts about some teachers needing to move out of their comfort zone and into new areas of the curriculum. For three weeks, I worked on a master schedule, which I released to the faculty two days before the end of the year.

The response of the faculty to my leadership judgment call is not printable. I created a firestorm of criticism and angst—a firestorm that I could have avoided. To say the least, in making this call, I had not acted responsibly toward those to whom I was accountable.

What went wrong, other than I had violated every principle of exercising good judgment? I had made some fatal mistakes:

- I failed to *tie the action to results*. What student achievement results were to improve as a result of this leadership action?

- I failed to *empathize* with others and anticipate their responses to the additional burden I was creating.

- I failed to *listen*. Actually, I failed to *ask* anyone in my N-S-E-W sphere if they thought this was a good judgment.

- I failed to *understand that leadership is a team sport*, and good judgment must be exercised by and involve everyone, especially the leader.

- I failed to *gather local knowledge* about why the current two-preparation system made sense to our faculty, even though it made no sense to me at the time.

- I had failed to identify any research that would support my decision.

In this instance, my "intuition" failed because I failed, as a leader, to blend deliberate and thoughtful analysis into my judgment, and I failed to take into account the thoughts and feelings of others.

Within a few weeks, I created a new master schedule and began discussions with key departmental leaders about how to best begin expanding the faculty's curricular awareness without causing shock waves to ripple though the school. I also personally apologized to my entire staff at an end-of-the-year meeting. This was a hard-won lesson about the importance of input from those who will be affected by leadership decisions. I could have avoided the problems I created by following some important criteria for making good judgment calls. To reiterate, the criteria are:

1. **Tie any decision-making action to results.** What student achievement results do you expect to improve because of this leadership action?

2. **Empathize with others.** What will be the expected reality placed on others? Anticipate their responses to the additional expectations from their perspective.

3. **Take time to listen.** Field-test and ask those in your N-S-E-W sphere if they think the decision-making action will result in good judgment. Don't assume you know best.

4. **Create a good judgment team.** Good judgment must be exercised by and involve everyone. Who on your team can you trust in the decision-making and good judgment process?

5. **Gather all the facts.** What are motivational factors for faculty and staff? How does the judgment for decision making connect to the shared vision and values? How will these factors be announced as part of the decision-making process? How will the judgment call affect those closest to the action? Is there any educational research that supports the decision-making action?

Ultimately, it becomes your responsibility to "make the call" and exercise good judgment after reviewing the data from others and gathering the necessary input from stakeholders. You *serve* by taking the time to pursue the input before making the judgment calls. These may not be popular calls, but they will be *good* calls if and when they lead to "things getting better."

Real servant leadership begins when you have taught the values of the organization so well that each and every team also begins to make good judgments—judgments based on the belief that the resulting actions will lead to improved results. In a professional learning community, ultimately, all decisions are judged by their results.

### Be "Interruptible"

Are you interruptible? Do you have an open-door policy? Do you follow the rules that apply to everyone else, even the students? Are you willing to do *any* task in the school, even the lowliest of tasks? Are you filled with a sense of self-importance? Are you too busy to be helpful, especially to those in your south grid? Think about the definition of service and sharing again. The responsibility of the leader is to *demonstrate personal accountability . . . to all who may be affected by your thoughts, words, actions, and inactions.*

A great example of this leadership practice occurred during my second year as superintendent. Due to a variety of software issues, the wrong schedule was presented to 2,500 of our students on opening day—a major crisis for the student services department and the school. At issue was our leadership response. Who would be willing to serve outside of the guidelines of their contract? Who would be willing to have their workday interrupted and help hand-schedule students into the right classes? In a typical Stevenson response—at a time of crisis—many faculty and staff signaled, "I am not 'too busy' at the start of a school year to be helpful," "I am not 'too big' to say that's not my job," or "I am not 'too important' to pitch in." For three days and nights, many of our faculty, administrators, and counselors worked tirelessly in every free moment possible to resolve the crisis.

The service and sharing spirit of our adults was rewarding. And for a brief moment, it highlighted our collaborative nature to do what is best for students. Yes, there were some adults who refused to help. There were some adults who saw the scheduling nightmare as "not my problem," who made it clear they were "not interruptible." I made sure to talk with those individuals privately after the crisis was over. Bottom line, is there no routine task you wouldn't do in your school, *even if no one were looking?* That is the mark of a servant leader.

There is a more subtle side to this serving practice as well. It is the way you as a leader convey the importance of those you serve *to* those you serve. As superintendent, besides personally modeling service and sharing, one of the primary ways I led a culture of service was to be sure to teach it to others. I have observed many teachers, parents, and administrators fail to be fully present when anyone in their N-S-E-W sphere needed to see them. They communicated, indirectly, that they were preoccupied with more important things or people—this meeting was just an interruption. How hard is it for others to be able to meet with you, and when they do meet with you, are you fully there for them? When they are with you, are you serving them by being with them, in that moment? Just ask. They'll let you know. Like the time my then fourteen-year-old son said, "Dad, you listen to us. You just don't hear what we are saying."

Over the years, one method I used to be more fully present was to take notes during conversations with someone. I found that taking notes helped me to slow down my own thought patterns, create a visual picture of the conversation, be more attentive to what the other person was saying, and think through follow-up questions to seek greater personal understanding, especially once the conversation had ended. What method works best for you?

## Establish Personal Intimacy

The leaders who have the most influence on you are those closest to you. To really serve and influence others requires authentic closeness, and closeness requires making an enemy of superficiality—and the enemy of superficiality is intimacy. For the PLC leader, intimacy is measured by the closeness of your relationships with your N-S-E-W people, as well as your closeness to the quality of work or competence you and your peers provide.

Not surprisingly, barriers to relational intimacy at work include arrogance, legalistic contracts, and orientation toward self or ego rather than toward the good of the team. Those who refuse to be seriously accountable for the results of their work and actions avoid intimacy—on purpose. It is why some leaders and teachers prefer isolation—no intimacy required.

PLC leaders understand team relationships that honor the shared vision and values that enable the professional learning community to move toward intimacy. Legalistic relationships based on contracts about working conditions generally are not designed to engender intimacy. Ardent proponents of such relationships work against intimacy by supporting strict adherence to rules and regulations that protect mediocrity, minimal performance, and hidden practice. Legalistic relationships rarely move teams of people to do great things. To create a relational culture, design meaningful relationships about *why* you do the work. Intimacy brings meaning to your leadership work far beyond "the students I teach" or "the adults I lead," and opens the door to reciprocal influences: north, south, east, and west.

How do you build intimacy? Max De Pree (1989) provides insight in *Leadership Is an Art*:

> How can we begin to build and nurture intimacy? Well, one way to begin is by asking questions and looking for answers. How does the company [school] connect with its history? What business is it in? Who are the people and what are their relationships with one another? How does the company [school] deal with change and conflict? Most important, perhaps, what is their vision of the future? Where are they going? What do they want to become? Leaders are obliged to think about these questions. Both the act and the art of leadership, if we are to be intimate with our work, demand this. (p. 61)

De Pree's words, when I first read them years ago, clarified for me one of the distinctive features of PLC leadership. PLC leaders are intimate with their work. I wanted to be intimate with my work. I wanted it to really matter. How about you? How does your area of school leadership connect with its history? How well does your school respond to change, conflict, and adversity? How well are you leading by asking questions and letting other provide the answers? Are you starting to rethink what it means to be intimate with your work? Ultimately, you decide how real intimacy will develop through the "quality of service" value created by your work together. In successful PLCs, all adults come to work in order to serve the growth and improvement of others.

Servant leadership that is more intimate and socially connected presents challenging territory and requires knowing how to influence others without being dictatorial. Unfortunately, this aspect of professionalism is often overshadowed in the selection of PLC administrators, academic coaches, and team leaders, whose appointments are typically based on other skills such as content knowledge and efficient school management. I am not saying these qualities are unnecessary; rather, they are simply not sufficient. Included in the PLC leaders' collection of influence skills is the capacity to understand the individual differences and communication skills of those they are leading. Meeting faculty members and fellow colleagues "where they are at" emotionally is based on equal parts advocacy and inquiry—and that takes a heavy dose of humility. Effective PLC leaders are able to evoke an emotional response and empathize with those in their sphere of influence. Yet PLC leaders also communicate a sense of urgency and tenacity for the vision work at hand. It is another paradox. Maintain intimacy and understanding by getting close to others, yet keep an appropriate social distance to keep your eye on the bigger perspective.

## Build Communities of Practice

As Kouzes and Posner (2006) point out, "Only leaders who serve, earn commitment. The purpose of leaders is to mobilize others to *serve a purpose* . . . and the purpose comes first" (p. 17, emphasis added). There it is: a culture of service nurtures commitment: adult *commitment around a purpose.* Adult sharing must occur around a purpose, and the singular purpose of a professional learning community is improved student learning.

You cannot have a highly effective sharing culture without a leadership style of serving others. The key to sustaining a coherent cycle for the continuous growth and improvement of all adult teams is the complete acceptance of mutual ownership in the discipline of sharing. Failure to share with anyone is an ego problem, an "I'm not in the work for the greater good of all" problem, and it is one of the greatest PLC leadership problems that you must confront.

Developing the relational capacity of others is best sustained by a sharing culture in the context of the teachers' workplace. Monitoring the effective sharing within teams is one of the most important leadership tasks for you to exercise, and ultimately for the PLC team to exercise under its own will.

There are, of course, numerous sources of experts on the subject of high-performing collaborative teams. Two excellent sources are *The Wisdom of Teams* by Jon R. Katzenbach and Douglas K. Smith (1993), and *Change, Lead, Succeed* by Linda Munger and Valerie von Frank (2010). My intent in mentioning these resources is not to study what professional learning community teams are to do, or to further support why they are so critical to school success. Rather, these resources outline the *process* of how you as a leader can *evaluate* the quality of the capacity building for the N-S-E-W teams you lead, participate in, and help to develop.

In *The Six Secrets of Change* Fullan (2008) provides an excellent description of the goals of capacity building with insight into how we might assess whether teams are improving. According to Fullan:

> Capacity building concerns competencies, resources, and motivation. Individuals and groups are high in capacity if they possess and continue to develop knowledge and skills, if they attract and use resources (time, ideas, expertise, money) wisely, and if they are committed to putting in the energy to get important things done collectively and continuously (ever learning). This is a tall order in complex systems, but it is exactly the order required. (p. 57)

Fullan's insight suggests you must monitor evidence that all members of the faculty and/or administrative teams demonstrate increasing personal and collective knowledge, motivation, and expertise. As well, there should be evidence that team members are becoming more confident in sharing knowledge without fear of judgment or reprisal from other team members or those in their N-S sphere. Fullan claims that "capacity building trumps judgmentalism" (p. 58); I couldn't agree more. As a PLC leader in the school or district, *your* tolerance of any form of judgmental behavior by those in your N-S-E-W sphere is catastrophic.

It is impossible to build effective communities of practice if teams of adults are not clear about the difference between exercising judgment and being judgmental. *Judgment* is the analysis of whether or not your standards and expectations for work performance were met (Stage 5 of the continuous cycle of improvement). It is best when those judgments occur at the tier 1 (self) and tier 2 (lateral) levels of accountability. It helps if the team members pass judgment together, without being judgmental of or blaming one another as individuals. As Collins (2009) suggests, effective teams conduct "autopsies without blame, mining wisdom from painful experiences" (p. 78).

Being *judgmental* occurs when, as an individual or as a member of a team, you think of yourself as morally superior to the lesser acts of others. Judgmentalism rules with fear, out of hubris and insecurity. It will quickly derail attempts to build relational capacity. As the PLC leader, you must be on the alert for it, and you must stop it in its tracks—immediately. Judgmentalism is a cancer to your school culture and your personal success as a PLC leader.

Respect for the craft knowledge and wisdom of those closest to students, the faculty and staff, is a positive attribute of professional learning communities. Obviously, respect is essential to sustaining effective communities of practice. Building on this culture of respect is a realistic way to determine the effectiveness of the communities. Five criteria provide a basis for examining the effectiveness of your various teams in communities of practice:

1. Does the team often discuss its failures? Does the team view failures as opportunities to learn or to make improvements in the future? How much does the team learn from its failures?

2. Does the team tolerate its members being judgmental? Does it tolerate insults? Anger? Fear tactics, put-downs, rolling of the eyes, and use of the words *but* or *they* in comments like, "But your idea will never work because they won't let us . . ."?

3. Does the team use an ongoing cycle of continuous improvement to reflect on results and share what worked and didn't work? Do team members understand that team learning is an ongoing process?

4. Does the team continuously disperse learning and share with others? Does the sharing of craft knowledge play a key role in every team meeting?

5. Does the team expand beyond its current group knowledge to learn from and use outside trusted sources of information, including national organizations, other schools, respected research, and outside experts? Does the team ask every month, every year, is there a better way to do this?

These questions should be completed and answered by every level of teams in your sphere of influence and definitely as an end-of-year reflection. Results of the team member reflections on these questions are subsequently used as part of a formative cycle of learning for the team. You and the team leaders can use the results to improve the *process* of team member participation the following semester or year. (Visit **go.solution-tree.com/plcbooks** to download the *Building Communities of Practice* worksheet to guide your reflection.)

*Collective*, not individual, brainpower must become the rule for successful communities of practice. Collective effort leads to information sharing, sound decision making, credible judgment, and team autonomy. Such effort trumps individual isolation, judgmentalism, and selfishness every single time. As you build effective communities of practice, the N-S-E-W serving effect eventually wears out the final line of resistors, or what Anthony Muhammad (2009) refers to as the "Level Four Fundamentalists":

> There is only one real solution for Level Four Fundamentalists, strict monitoring. Leaders must send the message that the standards have changed, and the only way someone will be allowed to be comfortable is through compliance with the new school paradigm. (p. 96)

The new school paradigm becomes "All adults practice service and sharing with one another around the vision and values of the school." Your mission, as a leader, *is to teach and establish* an E-W lateral accountability system that supports compliance with team work, creates a culture of serving one another, and ensures the vision prevails. Student achievement depends on it. Your E-W accountability system should provide a very narrow focus for the work of the team and the PLC leader. In turn, such a system will bring greater coherence and depth to your work.

Ron Gallimore and his associates (2009) conducted research that showed why some schools (scale-up schools) had dramatic gains in student achievement and others did not. The research findings indicate:

- Absent a common task immediately relevant to each teacher's own classroom, it is difficult to create and sustain the kind of inquiry cycle observed in the scale-up schools. In elementary school programs, grade-level teams fulfill this function. The secondary level has been most successful when teachers are organized into course or subject-area teams such as seventh-grade pre-algebra or ninth-grade English.

- To be successful, teacher learning teams need to set and share goals that are immediately applicable to their classrooms. Without such goals, teacher learning teams will drift toward superficial discussions and truncated efforts to test alternative instruction, assessment, and engagement methods.

Your Gallimore takeaway? Each year, the PLC leader must work with each team to keep team members focused on a small number of tasks that are *immediately relevant to the classroom.*

## Build the Relational Capacity of the Team

We are social human beings by nature. You are wired to connect with others. Actually, every adult and every student is wired to connect with others. No one benefits from the stress and inequity caused by isolated learning and decision making. And yet many in our profession would prefer to just be left alone. Why? Daniel Goleman (2007) points out in *Social Intelligence* that "nourishing relationships have a beneficial impact on our health, while toxic ones can act like slow poison to our bodies" (p. 5). Goleman further notes that "how we connect with others has unimagined significance. . . . In effect, being chronically hurt and angered, or being emotionally nourished by someone we spend time with daily over the course of years can refashion our brain" (2007, p. 11). Successful PLCs provide an environment in which nourishing relationships flourish, and isolation is not preferred.

Your role as a PLC leader in developing the relational capacity of a team is twofold. Initially, you teach the norms and behaviors necessary for team participation. Then, you extend the training into the *relationship capacity* skills necessary to be *part of* a successful team.

One way to develop the latter skill in others to is to have team members examine their team history. Our leadership teams routinely (every two years or so) participated in a "knowing your history" team exercise. How did the team come to exist? More importantly, what were the major and significant events, or defining moments, in the team's history? Each member of our team was required to submit a historical timeline describing significant events and years. Team members were asked to mark each significant event as positive or negative from their individual perspectives.

The sharing of each team member's timeline is an important exercise in relationship building. Is there consensus or disagreement regarding events that shaped each team member over the years? If positive, how can these events be repeated for the benefit of the team? If negative, what were the lessons learned? Is there a way to avoid the negative events in the future? What are the relational elements that have defined your team's culture of sharing?

Searching your team's history can yield profound insights about the *why* behind current collaborative relationships in six key areas. You can use the following questions on the six areas to nurture healthy discussions about the relational capacity and intimacy level of every team. Each team member should answer the critical questions individually before the team meets to discuss variant views and understandings.

1. **Motivation for becoming a professional learning community team.** Do team members primarily relate to one another out of compliance, or out of self-efficacy and the desire to be part of a team? Does the team understand the importance of its work as a team—focus on improved student learning? Do team members display *interdependence*?

2. **Attitudes toward collaboration.** Do team members tend toward getting things done together? Do they tend to be trusting or suspicious of each other? Do they respect organizational structure or do as they please? Are team members laid-back or high-strung, optimistic or pessimistic, cheerful or dismal, enthusiastic or reserved, isolated or participatory?

3. **Tier 2 E-W lateral accountability.** Do the team members work well together? Challenge one another? Hold one another accountable to the agreed-upon action for the vision and values of the school and the grade-level or course content? Encourage one another? Care about one another? Know the emotional lives of one another?

4. **Work ethic.** Does the team have a strong or weak work ethic? When things get tough and stressful, do members rise to the occasion or flail about? Do they support or push back against team decisions? Do they attack good ideas and explain why they won't work, or do they offer constructive solutions?

5. **Energy plus or minus.** Is the team primarily high or low maintenance? Do small annoyances create chaos, or does it take a lot to aggravate the team? Does the team add energy or drain energy from its members?

6. **Responses to conflict.** Does the team handle conflict and conflict resolution well? Do team members avoid difficult conversations and people, or are they proactive in seeking solutions and addressing the conflict with grace?

   (Visit **go.solution-tree.com/plcbooks** to download the worksheet *Knowing Your Team History*.)

As your leadership teams respond to the new and required form of professional development in a PLC—learning *with* colleagues—working through these questions will improve their ability to serve one another during times of great progress as well as times of conflict. Your leadership role is to foster relational capacity among various teams, recognize when it is low, and if so, provide *immediate feedback* for improvement.

In my area of school leadership, I realized very early in the team development process that we needed a clear process for conflict resolution. Our team leaders worked together to develop an informal conflict resolution agreement that would become part of the team norms. We understood up front that every year there would be team conflict at some level. So, why not have a team adversity plan that kicks into action once conflict arose? We called this our "Care Enough to Confront" plan. (Visit **go.solution-tree.com/plcbooks** to download a reproducible version of this plan.) The plan consisted of seven guidelines team members could follow because they *cared enough to confront*:

1. **Confront ASAP.** When a relational breakdown occurs between two people on the team, address the issues immediately. Further delay and unresolved issues only complicate the team dynamics.

2. **Separate the team member from the wrong action.** Most team conflict issues are about a team member's action that undermines the work of the team: for example, failure to be on time, failure to complete an assigned portion of the work project on time, failure to contribute in a positive manner, failure to act on an agreed-upon project or lesson assessment. It is the team member's actions that need to be addressed, not the quality of the person.

3. **Give the team member the benefit of the doubt.** It is important not to assume you know why the person was late, failed to deliver the project, or didn't meet the deadline. Allow the person an opportunity to explain his or her actions.

4. **Avoid absolute words.** Avoid using such words as *always* and *never* ("You always let the team down," "You never show up on time," "You never contribute to our team"). These types of statements are rarely true and diminish the speaker's credibility.

5. **Avoid sarcasm.** Do not use phrases such as "I know you just think you are too good for us" or "Maybe if you would try just a bit harder

you could get it right next time" or "Well, our team knows what
you'll be doing while we work on this—nothing!"

6. **Tell the team member how you feel about what was done wrong.**
It is very important to let the team member know how his or her
actions made you and/or the team feel. How does the action impact
others? Often, offenders to the team norms and values do not fully
realize the emotional wake they leave behind because of their actions
or inactions in relation to team values and commitments.

7. **Keep a short account.** Every team encounters some adversity as
members debate and argue about important practices and methods
for the teaching and learning. Once the *care enough to confront* discussion is completed, everyone on the team must let it go, move on, and
keep a short mental account of the issue. Team members who harbor
long-term resentments will be toxic to the team's growth.

Confronting shortcomings and conflicts within the team will require your *willingness* to have tough conversations with certain people in your N-S-E-W sphere.
Tony Schwartz (2010) provides insight into the relational aspect of conflict:

> Leaders who avoid conflict often cause more harm than those
> who are more direct. The key is to balance honesty with apprecia-
> tion, always keeping in mind the value of the other person, even
> when being critical of a particular behavior. (p. 289)

Chances for serving and sharing success are increased when leaders try to measure the softer side of team sharing and pay attention to the process of the team
communication.

## Measure and Teach the Softer Side of Team Sharing

About five years into our serious pursuit of professional learning community
teams and team sharing, I would make the rounds among all of our teams and
observe the way in which they shared information and ideas with one another.
As a PLC leader, you must not only monitor classroom practice and teaching, but
also serve the teams you lead by monitoring their meetings and providing feedback on how well they serve and share with one another. Remember, in a professional learning community culture, everything is transparent, and observing your
team meetings is a practice expected of the PLC leader.

John Kotter and Lorne Whitehead (2010) describe a framework for identify-
ing three primary forms of verbal attacks often used by team members that can

undermine the distribution and discussion of good ideas. PLC leaders should be on the lookout for verbal attacks that fall into the following categories of response:

1. We don't need your idea, because the "problem" it solves doesn't exist.

2. Okay, the problem exists, but your solution isn't a good one.

3. Okay, a problem exists, and your solution is a good one, but it will never work *here!*

These "implicit attitudes of the attacker" (Kotter & Whitehead, 2010, p. 106) highlight typical communication attacks team members may unwittingly use. These responses assume that each idea is in competition with another, but in fact competing ideas can *all* be very good ideas. The question for the team to focus on isn't why any of the ideas won't work. The question to answer is which of these ideas can serve the greater good—or is there a way to combine our ideas to better serve the greater good?

Dealing with controversy arising from such kinds of attacks is why we began a process of using an observer to monitor the conversation and communication tone of our more difficult PLC team meetings. Notice how two of Kotter and Whitehead's categories use the word *but.* This is one of the reasons we outlawed that word as part of our verbal conversations and replaced it with the word *and.* We wanted our PLC conversations to sound more like this: "Okay, that problem does exist, *and* how can we use your solution to also address the concern of [fill in the blank]?" I have often referenced this type of thinking as "making hot fudge sundaes." How can we take two divergent ideas (I want a cold dessert, and you want a hot dessert) and meld them to make a better whole? One of our PLC team goals was to work hard to take divergent thoughts and combine them to make new and more meaningful ideas.

Many of our mathematics and science teams would meet in the cafeteria during their team meeting time, and I would rotate from team to team. Occasionally I would record a session and send the digital file to the team leader for reflection on the effectiveness of the team's sharing. One of the main concerns in my specific area of school leadership (the hard sciences) is that there was often a lack of feelings expressed or acknowledged in the meeting. Sometimes the team leaders would dominate the work of the team without regard for how it was processed.

So how can we measure the effectiveness of the process for sharing and creating knowledge within our teams? David Meador's writing in the *Dance of Change* (Senge et al., 1999) suggests four ways that intentional team practices can be measured for accountability to the "soft side" of team service and sharing (p. 312). Meador's suggestions, highlighted in bold, are explained here in more detail:

1. **Does the team use open inquiry about difficult issues?** If you survey team members or observe their behavior, can they tell stories of breakthroughs and moments when they became closer as a team? Is the number of positive stories shared with the team about overcoming difficult issues in class increasing over time? Do team members take risks about what is and isn't working for them and share the results in front of one another?

2. **Does the team leader treat team members with dignity and respect?** Is there a hostile team environment? Are data available that could be independently verified and even tracked using an outside observer to identify words that show disrespect for others? Has the team established behavioral norms, and do members respect those norms? Do they listen without interrupting? Does there appear to be evidence they can discuss issues and needs for resolution without being judgmental of one another? Does the team leader "call fouls" on team members who violate the norms—in a way that works and can be heard by others?

3. **Does the team use advocacy and inquiry for effective conversation?** Video or audio record some meetings, and conduct a word analysis. How many times do people say, "I propose we do this now" versus "Could you explain your reasoning?" or "Could you say more?" You could probably weight different phrases according to the level of advocacy versus inquiry. For example, "I don't know, what do you think?" would indicate a high degree of openness. "That's not the way we do it around here" might indicate a low tendency to integrate new ideas. Is each person on the team given an opportunity advocate a position and be heard? Is the word *but* used a lot to repudiate the thoughts of others? Such information can provide valuable insights into team communications.

4. **Is there genuine care for the collegial community?** On some level, does there appear to be a commitment from everyone on the team to the question, should I get involved with my colleagues in an E-W sphere of learning? This is a question of commitment to the belief in and value of a professional learning community. When those in your E-W spheres genuinely demonstrate care for one another—when they

embrace, through service, the emotional lives of others—meaningful adult learning and sharing become the norm.

Measuring your N-S-E-W teams using these process boundary markers will give you insight into why certain teams seem more intimate (and judgmental in a softer way), and other teams seem more judgmental (in a harsher way) and struggle with sharing. Observing and surveying team process skills regularly—monthly, midyear, and at the end of the year—enables a leader to determine the level of service orientation within each team.

## *Choose to Be an Inequity Eraser*

Until recently, there has been a mystifying silence in the PLC leadership literature about how the discipline of service and sharing—hallmark qualities of all teachers and leaders in a professional learning community—serves as an inequity eraser for the social injustices caused by isolated decision making and the resultant wide variance in student learning experiences.

Decisions made in isolation or as a result of teacher learning team dysfunction affect the rigor of daily classroom task selection choices, ongoing rigor for assessment task selection, and instructional lesson design practices. These noncollaborative decisions are primary contributors to this variance. Inequities can be seen throughout the K–12 curriculum teaching and learning experience, unfortunately. At least six areas of inequity are created by the failure of grade-level and course-based faculty teams to work together within a serving and sharing culture. As PLC leaders, it is our task to attack these inequities with passion and persistence.

1. **Access inequity.** This inequity is seen in who gets access to the school's various academic programs once tracking begins in fifth grade and beyond. Most kids are locked into a permanent track as early as sixth and seventh grade. How is it decided who gets into and out of a level or track?

2. **Task selection inequity.** The selection and rigor of tasks and experiences performed by students each day in class reveals inequities in the quality of lesson planning from teacher to teacher.

3. **Formative assessment inequity.** Task selection and level of rigor of daily in-class prompts and tasks used by teachers to assess student understanding also vary, as do rigor and task selection for homework assignments, rules for makeup work, and the depth and quality of teacher feedback on formative work.

4. **Summative assessment inequity.** Inequities can emerge in the rigor in task selection that teachers or teacher teams use for unit tests and quizzes. How do you, as the school leader, define high-quality assessments for each academic discipline, grade level, or course? How high is your tolerance level for tests and exams that either do not meet the prescribed standards or vary widely in task rigor from teacher to teacher of the same course or grade level?

5. **Grading inequity.** The grading of all assessments, formative learning, and effective feedback loops is one of the areas of greatest inequity. Assessment tasks must be discussed and agreed upon by all team members to arrive at an implementation of common practice.

6. **RTI inequity.** How variant, swift, and complete is the intentional and collective team response to instruction and intervention on all aspects of the academic programs you lead? How well do your responses demonstrate evidence that both students and teachers are becoming reflective learners?

When you become skilled at exercising the discipline of service and sharing to resolve these inequities, you enable your N-S-E-W relationships to make the critical move from a being a "working group" to becoming an interdependent team. Katzenbach and Smith (1993) call this the "critical choice." The distinction between a working group and a true team is as follows: "A working group relies primarily on the individual contributions of its members for group performance, whereas a team strives for a magnified impact that is incremental to what its members could achieve in their individual roles" (p. 88). Teams attack the inequities and seek out "magnified impact" that is far greater than any individual could ever achieve.

As a school leader, you need *magnified impact*. You need *teams*. You need your teams to be the smallest unit of change in the school or program. Your students need highly effective faculty grade-level or course-based teams that work diligently to erase the inequities created by the widely variant judgments that occur when teachers and administrators work in isolation or simple groups. Again, how do teams differ from working groups? *Team* members are willing to relate and rely on each other. More wisdom from Katzenbach and Smith (1993):

> [Teams] require both individual and mutual accountability. Teams rely on more than group discussion, debate, and decision; on more than sharing information and best practice perspectives; on more than a mutual reinforcing of performance standards.

> Without discrete team work-products produced through the joint,
> real contributions of team members, the promise of incremental
> or magnified performance impact goes untapped. (p. 90)

A team promises greater performance than a working group, but it also brings more risk. Becoming a team demands a leap of faith. Rugged individualists—and there are many, especially at the top—often instinctively believe in the adage "If you want a job done right, do it yourself." It is against their nature to rely on others. But you cannot contribute to real team performance without taking responsibility for your peers *and* letting your peers assume genuine responsibility for your actions.

Not taking the leap of faith to become a team has a high price in terms of the group's effectiveness. So does "faking" the leap of faith by participating in the team discussions, and then doing what you want regardless of the team decisions. If the team approach fails, "members do get diverted from their individual goals, work-products do not add significant value, costs do outweigh benefits, and people do resent the imposition on their time and priorities" (Katzenbach & Smith, 1993, p. 90).

Here's the point. Your leadership within the professional learning community— your ability to model service and sharing in yourself and then develop N-S-E-W leadership in others—will accomplish two great things. First, you will remove any barriers to participation in community. Second, you will open the doors to transparency and collective inspection of ideas and actions that create the six great inequities. To that end, you must be steadfast in the teaching of sharing as an organizational value. In the words of John Gardner (1988):

> As for leaders, their task is more demanding. They must not only
> have their own commitments, they must move the rest of us
> toward commitment. They call us to the sacrifices necessary to
> achieve our goals. They do not ask more than the community can
> give, but often ask more than it intended to give or thought it was
> possible to give. (p. 7)

Service and sacrifice. Meaningful relationships. Giving more than you thought you could give, but not too much. Personal humility and professional will. This is your leadership, your life, your serving and sharing legacy. You stretch those in your N-S-E-W sphere, but not so far you lose them. Doing this discipline well is both an art and a science. You train to get better at it, and you learn to get better though the lessons of each relational experience.

## *Accept Others*

One last caution: your growth in the discipline of service and sharing may not be fully realized if you limit your passion to passion for reaching student achievement goals. Your leadership life needs to be about so much more than just reaching those goals. It is about serving all those in your N-S-E-W sphere, including and especially yourself, in such a way that you and they reach their full leadership potential. Nothing else is good enough. The mark of great leaders is evidence that they achieved their full potential and helped others to do so as well. Did you support *and* encourage others to reach their full potential—every person, every adult in your N-S-E-W sphere, every single one? Robert Greenleaf hints at this leadership call to greatness:

> The interest and affection the leader has for his [or her] followers—and it is a mark of true greatness when it is genuine—is clearly something that the followers "haven't to deserve." I have known some great leaders; it has been my privilege to work for a few. Some, not all, had gruff, demanding, uncompromising exteriors, but deep down, inside all those I think as a great—no exceptions—was a thoroughly feminine aspect, reflected in their unqualified attitude of acceptance of their people ... because their followers felt accepted, they tended to perform beyond the limits they had set for themselves. Initially, they may have excelled to please their leader but eventually they did so to please themselves. (Frick & Spears, 1996, p. 310)

During the time I was superintendent, I struggled to accept the behavior of a particular faculty member. That person's behaviors and off-putting attitudes were hard for me to tolerate at times. It would be appropriate to say I considered this person an antagonist to me personally as well. And yet, I willed myself at times to lean into this person, to better understand the human story, to accept the person, even though I often needed to reject the actions. Shortly after I retired from Stevenson, I received a remarkable handwritten note from this individual thanking me for the time I had given during my tenure at the school, and letting me know that I would be missed. I honestly had no idea that there was an ounce of a grateful heart in this person. Our exchanges over the years had been rough and difficult. Lesson learned: you just never know how your words and actions impact others.

You know right now the people in your N-S-E-W sphere who perhaps "haven't behaved to deserve" your acceptance. No matter. Don't delay. Seek them out so they can reach their full potential and, in turn, serve others. It is your leadership task to help everyone to become an equity hero. It may take a long time with some—so serve them better. Lean into them *more* often. Give them no choice but to feel accepted by you as a person, even if you must reject their actions because of how they cause inequity to surface. Almost all of PLC leadership is a paradox. This is one, too. In the end, all they will really remember about you is how well you leaned into and listened to them. You will be a better leader for choosing to accept *all* of those in your leadership path, even those who eventually must be told their path must change. You can accept the person, even if you have to dismiss the person's behavior.

# Study Guide ▪ ▪ ▪ ▪ ▪

Visit **go.solution-tree.com/plcbooks** to download this study guide and the worksheets mentioned in it.

## *Examining My Leadership Perspective*

1. Which educational "thought leader" has had the greatest impact on your leadership life? In what ways has that person's thinking significantly influenced your leadership beliefs and actions? If possible, how might you let that person know how you feel?

2. How are you staying current with "new edge" information that provides the *technical* resources of leadership? What leadership books are you currently reading? How are you transferring knowledge from those resources to your leadership actions?

3. In a dozen or so words, how would you describe your primary *pursuit* as a PLC school leader? What is your number-one responsibility and priority right now?

4. Building and sustaining relationships is critical to a leader's effectiveness and success. What do you think are your strengths and limitations in the relationships you have with those leaders to your north? With your peers in the east and west spheres? With those you lead to your south? In what ways has the information in this chapter helped you to analyze those relationships? How has the information helped you to build the relational capacity of those individuals and teams within your sphere of influence? What information could you use in an effort to improve a relationship with a difficult colleague? Use *The N-S-E-W PLC Sphere of Influence Chart* to focus a team discussion about collegial relationships.

5. Identify the best team experience you have had as a PLC school leader. What aspects of team member communication made that experience positive and worthwhile?

## *Extending My Leadership Perspective*

1. Ask all your faculty teams to complete the *Building Communities of Practice* worksheet. How will you use the results to identify areas in need of improvement for building the knowledge capacity of the team? What resources will you draw upon to foster the team's growth?

2. Ask all your faculty teams to complete the *Knowing Your Team History* worksheet. What do the results reveal about the progress of your PLC

commitment to becoming a sharing community? For the weakest-performing PLC teams, which aspects of knowing your team history are in greatest need of improvement? What resources will you draw upon to make the necessary improvements?

3. School leaders have a major responsibility to eliminate inequity. What are the inequities that exist in your area of school leadership? To what extent do the administration, faculty, and staff acknowledge these inequities? Are the administration, faculty, and staff committed to addressing the issues surrounding these inequities? What plan do you have for solving problems caused by these inequities?

4. PLC leaders pursue an expanded leadership base. What are your plans for fostering an environment that supports a more distributed leadership?

5. What attributes must leaders possess (or acquire) to ensure that either "leadership by Barney the Dinosaur" or "leadership by Attila the Hun" does not characterize their performance? In your experience, have you encountered such leaders? If so, how did you deal with them at the time? As a result of studying this chapter, how would you deal with them now?

CHAPTER 4

*The Discipline of*

# Reflection and Balance

"A slow sort of country," said the Queen. "Now, here, you see, it takes all the running you can do, to stay in the same place. If you want to get somewhere else, you must run at least twice as fast as that!"

—Lewis Carroll

To become a fully engaged PLC leader, one who does not succumb to the intense and often urgent pace and expectations of the position, requires personal training in the discipline of *reflection and balance*. This means you fully engage at work, *and* you intentionally disengage in order to rest and renew. You have developed a sense and clear understanding of how to balance expenditure of your energy with time for renewing your energy. You understand that failure to do so will lead to the ultimate downside of leadership: *negative energy and negative relationships producing constant and sustained overload in your work-related tasks.* That is not the desired path of a PLC leader, and you don't arrive there suddenly. An "everything is urgent" pace facilitates a drift toward negative energy. Extraordinary PLC leaders learn how to check for and then stop the drift.

As a PLC leader, you can be busy, controlling your pace, or you can be in a hurry, letting the pace control you. You can lead and direct vision casting. You can turn that vision into action. You can create a culture of service and sharing. You can be a model in those disciplines—*if* you lead and participate in a balanced and reflective leadership life. The discipline of reflection and balance is defined as follows:

### The leadership work of intentionally and strategically engaging in and disengaging from high-energy activities

This discipline gives more emphasis to managing your personal energy than managing your personal time. In *The Power of Full Engagement,* authors James Loehr and Tony Schwartz (2003) make a strong case for protecting your energy: "Energy, not time, is the fundamental currency of high performance" (p. 4). Energy can be infinite; monitoring use of your energy is essential to your ability to lead your professional learning community at a sustained and high level every day, every month, every year.

Leaders often hold faulty assumptions about time, making it the culprit that causes many of their daily leadership problems. There is not enough time to do it all. No matter how much faster you move, or how much more you try to squeeze into your 24/7 world, it's still 24/7. There is no 25/8 tomorrow. Time is finite. We are a society that moves fast—fast food, fast cars, faster Internet speeds, fast cell phone networks, and technological applications that allow us to work and act faster—the faster, the better. In fact, there is pressure both to do everything fast, and to be the best—please! James Gleick, in his 2000 book *Faster: The Acceleration of Just About Everything*, says:

> We know something's happening, and we're beginning to sense what it is. We're speeding up; our technology is speeding up; our arts and entertainment and the pace of invention and change— it's all speeding up. And we care. If we don't understand time, we become its victims. (p. 1)

As a PLC leader, a major source of both your personal satisfaction and your vulnerability is the speed of your leadership world. Every day, your life at school places great demands on your time and your energy. The pace at which you lead is ultimately a paradox. On one hand, the quick pace serves to help you and those in your area of leadership to experience an incredible, vibrant, hope-filled work life. You get a lot done, and it feels good. On many days you just flat-out know that your work, your effort, and your leadership *matter*. You, like others, are motivated by the progress being made. On the other hand, you can also become victim to the speed of leadership demands. If you don't fully realize the impact of speed on your leadership capacity, there will be devastating effects on your ability to lead yourself as well as those in your N-S-E-W spheres.

To avoid the pitfalls of moving too fast, you can train yourself to manage your energy for full engagement within a fixed amount of time: daily, weekly, or even yearly. The discipline of reflection and balance is designed to provide insight into thinking and practices that will prevent you from sliding into the low-energy side of the leadership world. Since the culture of speed is not going to slow down soon (if ever), the responsibility for surviving in this culture rests with you. How do you manage the energy of your life so that you can keep the speed of PLC leadership under control and be fully engaged in your work life? Such control will require intentional action to achieve internal balance and stubborn refusal to succumb to the external forces that disturb that balance. Fully engaged PLC leaders pursue a well-ordered leadership life.

# Refusing to Multitask

If you are relentlessly in a hurry to get everything done, you have a speed problem. If you are noticing the time for deep and meaningful relationships with those in your N-S-E-W spheres slipping away, you have a speed problem. If you feel overwhelmed by your workload, you have a speed problem. Your leadership is becoming out of balance.

Invariably, this happens to *every* school leader some time during the school year. Eventually the speed of expectations, the pace of obligations, or the "simpler, better, faster" mantra catches up to you—as a school leader and as a human being. Your energy, your full engagement at work, starts to falter, and you just can't keep all of the plates spinning—at work or at home.

At some point, like the Red Queen in *Alice in Wonderland* (Carroll, 1955), "it takes all the running you can do, to stay in the same place" (p. 164). And if you want to achieve something better? Then "run at least twice as fast" (p. 164). Eventually, the demands wear on you and erode your ability to do your job well. A quiet fear sets in. How will you find the time to complete your observation walkthroughs, attend teacher team meetings, prepare for and attend district and building-level meetings, submit the task force report, attend various cocurricular events, prepare for your leadership team meetings, write your monthly updates, organize the school fundraiser with the students, guide school discipline, meet with parents, *and* be fully present for various one-to-one meetings with faculty, staff, and colleagues, *and* find time for your family at home?

At some point in the school year, although you may not outwardly show or verbalize your angst, you know you are losing the pace battle. You go into work earlier and stay later. You go to work on a day with almost no meetings scheduled on your calendar only to get hit with a series of crises, interruptions, and new projects. By the end of the day, you have worked as hard as humanly possible. You have done as many tasks at the same time as you could. You have nothing left in the tank, yet little was achieved on the to-do list. In fact, the list grew, and tomorrow you have an even longer day planned. You ask yourself, why did I decide to become a school leader? The Red Queen is lurking around the corner.

Since the pace of your leadership work can be relentless, a default solution for responding to the demands and regaining your balance is the modern notion of multitasking. You try to do more things at the same time as a way of catching up with your workday. Some of you might be multitasking right now. As you are reading these words, what else are you doing: Listening to music? Checking your cell phone for text messages and signal beeps for incoming email? Running a load of laundry? Wondering about an overdue phone call? Reviewing your child's homework? Checking that the DVR is taping a favorite program that you will watch later (using an app in your iPhone/BlackBerry/Droid/Palm/other handheld device)?

Doing many tasks at the same time—that is, *not* doing those tasks one at a time—*multitasking*—is a huge detriment to effective leadership. Increasingly, as you multitask more, you provide only shallow attention to your work and to the relational demands placed on you as a PLC leader. You fall into the trap of superficiality; you lose focus, and you lack depth. Tony Schwartz (2010), in *The Way We're Working Isn't Working*, quotes University of Michigan researcher David Meyer regarding training for efficient multitasking: "Except in rare circumstances, you can train [for efficient multitasking] until you are blue in the face and you'd never be as good as if you focused on one thing at a time. Period. That's the bottom line" (p. 185). Schwartz goes on to say:

> We create plenty of distractions for ourselves by juggling tasks, making ourselves perpetually available to others, opening several windows on our computers, and focusing on whatever feels most urgent at the moment without regard to whether what we are doing is really important. (p. 196)

In the early stages of PLC team development at Stevenson, multitasking was one of the more toxic aspects of our team meetings. At the administrative team level, our team members would come to the meetings with computers and handheld devices; they would check and return email, text message, and work on various projects throughout the team meeting. Although team members would appear to be engaged in the conversation around the agenda for the meeting, they were often distracted and failed to provide meaningful input. Eventually, in order to prevent the multitasking, we added a team norm that restricted the use of any electronics at team meetings except for the purpose of presentation or discussion. Ultimately, we had to forbid bringing any form of electronic device to the meeting. Not surprisingly, the quality of our team conversations improved as team members listened and responded more attentively to the tasks and issues on the agenda.

Literary critic William Deresiewicz (2010), in a 2009 speech to the plebe class of the U.S. Military Academy, provides further evidence that multitasking impairs your ability to think. He states:

> A study by a team of researchers at Stanford came out a couple of months ago. The investigators wanted to figure out how today's college students were able to multitask so much more effectively than adults. How do they manage to do it, the researchers asked? The answer, they discovered—and this is by no means what they expected—is that they don't. . . . And here's the really surprising finding: the more people multitask, the worse they are, not just at other mental abilities, but at multitasking itself.
>
> They [multitaskers] were worse at distinguishing between relevant and irrelevant information and ignoring the latter. In other words, they were more distractible. They were worse at what you might call "mental filing": keeping information in the right conceptual boxes and being able to retrieve it quickly. In other words, their minds were more disorganized. And they were even worse at the very thing that defines multitasking itself: switching between tasks. (p. 5)

The Stanford study revealed that your ability to transfer between many tasks, even if done one at a time during a meeting or within a day, erodes if you try to multitask during each of those activities. In other words, keep your leadership focus on one task at a time without interruption by other inputs. Schwartz (2010) states it like this: "Assume for a moment that you can learn to resist distraction and do one thing at a time . . . where ought you put it? In the service of what's most important" (p. 196). Thus, every day your PLC leadership energy should be directed to the service of *what's most important*. But how do you decide what is most important, especially on the days or in the weeks where you feel pulled in every direction all at the same time?

During the time I was superintendent, I asked our leadership team to participate in a task-focusing experience that I had been part of as a leader in my volunteer life. I asked each member of our leadership team to create a six-by-six list on a large note card. This list was to indicate each member's top six priority tasks that must be completed in the next six weeks (in our district, the school year was built on six-week terms, so that seemed a reasonable length of time). These tasks were to be so important that if not completed, our students, our faculty, and our programs would suffer. Team members were to attach to this list a brief plan as to how those tasks would be accomplished with focus and clarity.

Eventually, and this was the greatest learning experience for our team, we shared our six-by-six lists with one another and explained our rationale to one another. (This idea was also part of my leadership learning from my private volunteer work.) Our team members were often surprised to see where other members thought their energy should be placed in the service of what is really important. Over time, I believe this management tool helped us to prioritize and reprioritize our focus throughout the year on the tasks that would add the greatest value to our shared vision and student achievement goals. (Visit **go.solution-tree.com /plcbooks** to download the worksheet *Task Priority Management Tool*.)

One of the main dilemmas that course and grade-level teams of teachers face is their effort to fulfill the various demands of their own team agenda, as well as the administration's agenda given to them. In their efforts to meet these demands, they naturally start to multitask. They might begin a team meeting with three to five tasks they are expected to complete—all at once and with the same priority for completion. We tried to corral this problem by defining specific purposes for every teacher team meeting. We limited the number of tasks for discussion to no more than two or three items that focused on one major vision action—for example, formative assessment. Team meetings were designated to address *one* type of task: either carrying out an administrative assigned task, or working on assigned tasks generated by the teacher team. It was important to limit the focus of the team's work expectations. This "less is more" philosophy for team meetings became a priority and helped team members overcome limitations caused by too much multitasking.

# Using Technology *Strategically*

Technology, and all it represents, is a primary cause and contributor to the distraction and shallowness of your multitasking world. Technology presents an additional paradox for you. On one hand, access to technology blurs the lines of time spent at home, work, or travel. Your work can be, and is, with you at all times. It is so efficient and freeing to be able to answer email, enter blog posts, review your Facebook page, and return text messages at any time of the day or night—communicating with one and all of those in your N-S-E-W sphere. On the other hand, for all the convenience, this situation is also stressful, especially when you place no boundaries on your use of communication technologies. Modern expectations for the speed of return communication are exponential. There is no hiding. Gleick (2000) states it like this:

> Reading E-mail starts to feel like a forced march through a shade-less landscape. [An] explanation for this phenomenon is that people's expectations for what to do with the mail changes: when they get a little, they treat it as personal correspondence and consider each message and its reply carefully. When they get a lot, most messages immediately are fated for the Delete key. Users are constantly behind on upgrading their behavior on this curve of information neglect, so they constantly feel stressed. (p. 88)

All forms of required and available communication and social networking tools serve as either an energy *drain* or an energy *gain* depending on your disposition toward setting boundaries for use. The question is not whether you have *time* for social networking, for example, but whether you have the *energy* for it. Do you establish a consistent pattern for doing it well? Are you willing to use technology strategically?

The stress caused by the advance of technology lies in your inability to keep up with the volume of input received, the nature of the changing technology, and the boundaries you place on when and how you will use it. Facebook, Twitter, Delicious, LinkedIn, Digg, StumbleUpon, Bebo, Blogger, Webnews, WordPress and YouTube are just some of the current methods of communication available to school leaders. If used in an appropriate context, these tools might make certain aspects of your leadership life more efficient. They could save you and your grade-level or course-based learning teams time and feed into your energy for doing your work. But if keeping pace with technology drains the precious energy resources you have available for activities that require your focused attention, then the balance of your leadership life suffers. Technology creates an alluring illusion that multitasking is okay. You think, "I *can* be fully involved in a conversation with a colleague *and* answer that email or text." But you can't. You simply cannot think for yourself, much less think for others, when you are constantly interrupted by Facebook and

Twitter posts or distracted by YouTube videos or your iPad®. Technology is such an interrupter of our work and focus that we all need rules to keep the expectations of technology tasks under control.

A few years ago, a national task force that I was leading became so abusive around the use of email (in terms of the volume, tone, intent, expectations for response time, and inappropriate use of copying others as a way of punishment) that I convened a meeting of the committee for the express purpose of establishing email norms. These norms, once agreed upon, I expected all to follow. It took almost a year of monitoring the committee use of email as a communication tool—including some very difficult conversations with communication violators—before the technology served our purpose without distraction from our work. Have you established email or texting norms that your learning teams, at all levels of the school organization, are expected to follow?

The email norms we established helped our task force to rebuild trust and function more appropriately. How does the following list of norms or "email boundaries" compare to the ones established and used by your leadership team?

1. **Establish clear expectations for email response time.** Do not expect emails you send to be responded to immediately. Do expect emails to be responded to within 24 hours.

2. **Always be polite. Do not use CAPITAL letters.** It is like shouting at other team members. Do not use a caustic or sarcastic tone. Do not complain about team members or the team's work. If you have a complaint, call the person. Do say thank you at the end of each email. Do use a greeting at the start of the message that acknowledges the person's name.

3. **Never use the blind copy (BCC) function.** A successful team must be transparent. If you have a concern or need to CC someone, then make sure everyone in the email knows who has been informed on the issue. Do CC only those people who really need to know.

4. **Keep emails short.** Do not send long emails concerning multiple issues. Do send emails that are crisp and to the point. Do be clear about the purpose of the email. Is it FYI and needs no response? Does the recipient need to provide input or take action?

5. **Seek permission to forward an email.** Do not forward an email you have received without permission to do so from the sender. The

sender may have written you a private message that he or she was not intending for others to see. Do be sensitive to the length of email you choose to forward to others.

(Visit **go.solution-tree.com/plcbooks** to download the worksheet *Dos and Don'ts for Email Use*.)

The pressure to "go higher tech" will not go away, but the changes in technology can become assets that support effective management of your leadership activities. However, technology should *not* come first, nor should it rule your leadership life. The overwhelming presence of technology can be tamed when you recognize and accept that it is subservient to the vision of your school and your school leadership. With this understanding, you can use technology strategically for specific purposes, within reasonable time frames. Where you are headed is more important than how fast technology can take you there. The tools of the social networking and media world will be only as good as the direction and vision of school improvement where they are applied.

Uncritical use of technology and excessive multitasking can contribute to a relentless onslaught of tasks that increasingly detract from your effectiveness as a leader. When this happens, you may discover that you are infected with *hurry sickness*, a term coined by cardiologist Meyer Friedman. Defined by WordSpy (McFedries, 2010), hurry sickness is "a malaise where a person chronically feels short of time, and so tends to perform every task faster and to get flustered when encountering any kind of delay" (p. 1). You can control or eradicate hurry sickness from your life if you understand its essential elements. (Visit **go.solution-tree .com/plcbooks** to download the *Hurry Sickness Checklist*.)

# Avoiding Excuses

Making excuses and blaming others (external factors) for your inability to get things done are sure signs that you—or those in your sphere of influence—are drifting into an energy crisis. Author James Loehr (2007) highlights this issue as "faulty assumption thinking" (p. 70) and provides insight into how leaders—at all levels of the school organization—tell themselves terrific excuses for why they do *not* need to plan strategically for a life of reflection and balance. These faulty assumptions can inadvertently lead to a victim mindset that you probably would not tolerate in others. More importantly, in the aggregate these excuses form a consistent pattern of "no accountability" half-truths that allow you to justify your leadership drifting into an energy crisis. Faulty assumptions can become pervasive within a professional learning community unless you as a leader work to eliminate them. Of course, PLC leaders themselves are not immune to making excuses. Here are examples of faulty assumptions that should be avoided at all costs:

- *Our students can't learn because they don't show up for class, they don't attend to the support we provide, and they don't care. What do you expect us to do?*

- *Most of our team problems stem directly from all of the stress placed on us by the principal. We'd be more responsible and engaged as teachers and as a team without that pressure.*

- *As a principal, the only way I can meet PLC expectations is to work longer and harder. The central-office demands are relentless.*

- *I must constantly check my email, my text messages, and my blog at home because as an academic coach I am responsible for a lot of people, and they need immediate responses.*

- *My teaching day controls me—not the opposite. I'm not the boss of anything. I have no control. I just do what they tell me to do—it's more, more, more. And now they want me to be part of a team?*

- *I invest most of my energy in the classroom and not with my team. I'm doing it all for the students, anyway, and the team doesn't really need my "stuff" or me.*

- *The team drags me down. Working on my own is my right, and no one can take that away from me. What right does the team have to tell me what to do?*

- *It's okay that I am not spending a lot of time observing my teachers teach and learning more about their needs. I run a very well-managed school, and the faculty understands that is what is most important.*

- *It's okay with my family members when I come home from work exhausted and disengaged. They appreciate all that I do for the school.*

- *I can get away with not passing assessments back to my students right away. They understand. Someday I have to significantly change the way I grade, but I still have time to figure it out.*

- *Taking care of myself physically is a luxury I can't afford right now. I devote what little time and energy I have to the areas of my life that matter most—my family and my job.*

Can you see how thinking like this, being consumed by excuses, can lead to leadership imbalance? Imbalanced thinking can send you spiraling into an energy freefall with little or no time to be effective because you are distracted, tired, and unable to keep all those work, family, and health "plates" spinning.

If you spend time in serious reflection about how you are doing, you can penetrate the veneer of these excuses. The barriers imposed by excuse making will fall, and your leadership life will assume more balance. "No one else who had my current job, my current home situation, or my personal life situation could find happiness, either" is a wonderful, but delusional, barrier to hide behind.

Why do adults tend to blame others, especially the mysterious "they," to justify their faulty assumptions? It is so much easier to just say, "*They* won't let us do this," "*They* are making us do this," or "*They* just don't understand our problems." One quick way to check the temperature of your PLC leadership life is to observe for the frequency with which *they* is used in team meetings or conversations.

In my work, eventually, we had to banish the use of *they* throughout our various learning teams. We had to call out every stakeholder group every time the word *they* was used. Who exactly are they? Central office? The administration? The teacher learning team? The faculty and staff in general? The students? The parents? Who, exactly, won't let you do something, is making you do something, or doesn't understand your needs? PLC cultures have no tolerance for the faulty assumption thinking allowed by the use of the word *they*.

Loehr (2007) refers to the tendency toward faulty assumption thinking as the "because I can syndrome" (p. 74). Why do I check emails while on vacation? Why do I text during family dinner? Why do I interrupt a conversation to take another call or return a text message? Why do I work every night until midnight? Why do I answer my cell phone during my daughter's concert? Why do I skip that afternoon workout? Why do I miss breakfast (other than coffee) every morning? Why do I blame others for my problems? *Because I can.* No one is telling you how to use and manage the energy of your life. Can you identify any current pattern of behavior or faulty thinking in your leadership life in which you suffer from the *because I can* syndrome? You may not have slowed down enough lately to be able to identify if you do—that's where the reflection part of this leadership discipline comes in.

*Every* school leader I know has this issue. I suspect that, at one time or another, you too have taken on too many tasks and become overwhelmed. The demands of managing work, family, and health make it impossible not to skirt the edges of faulty assumptions. Eventually, one of those areas, if not all three, begins to suffer. Becoming aware of faulty assumption thinking in your daily experiences and any tendency to make personal excuses to rationalize your leadership behavior is a first step toward denying the energy drain often caused by the *because I can* (get away with it without being challenged) syndrome. Take the time to ask yourself, are there any *because I can*s I need to address as soon as possible?

# Paying Attention to Students *and* Adults

As a PLC leader, you often fall into the *because I can* trap due to the sense that you are not keeping up with all the "stuff" on your leadership plate. "The hurrier I go, the behinder I get" is a well-known phrase that is often associated with Lewis Carroll's *Alice in Wonderland*. A modernized version might be "The faster I go, the shallower I get." In other words, when your leadership energy is low, you are much less likely to invest the quality time and care necessary to truly love those in your N-S-E-W sphere (including your family). Fullan (2008) states it like this:

> If you build your organization by focusing on your customers [students and parents] without making the same careful commitment to your employees [faculty and staff], you won't succeed for long. And we have all seen the opposite: the organization that seems to run for the benefit of the employees, with the customer perceived as an intrusion. Neither will do. . . . The key is in enabling employees to learn continuously and to find meaning in their work and in their relationship to coworkers and to the company as a whole. (pp. 11–12)

The last sentence deserves more attention. It provides a hint as to how PLC leaders are to *think* about how effectively their efforts are directed to the well-being of colleagues. Do your actions allow every teacher and staff member to:

- Learn continuously (participate in deep learning teams)
- Find meaning and purpose in his or her work (formulate a great vision)
- Find meaning and purpose in relationships (show team interdependence, care, grace, and respect)
- Find meaning and connection to the school (demonstrate love of the school he or she works for)

In other words, do the faculty and staff *love* to work in your district, at your school, or in your programs? Do they experience the full engagement and energy that call them to the PLC commitments necessary for meaningful, relevant teaching and student learning? Do they experience optimal learning and growth? For your area of school leadership, are the needs of the faculty and staff *as important as* the needs of the students?

Fullan (2008) later asserts, "Loving students and faculty equally can be done such that everyone benefits" (p. 26). This observation is critical for a fully engaged PLC leader. You must be fully engaged for your students as well as your faculty, staff, and colleagues in your N-S-E-W sphere. Attentiveness to one cannot be sacrificed at the expense of the other. One of the faulty leadership assumptions in a PLC culture is the belief that vision actions that are best for the faculty and staff will be counterproductive to doing what is best for the students. As a school leader, it is tempting here to submit to the "tyranny of OR." The faulty assumption thinking goes like this:

> I either pay attention to the faculty and staff, and give them the freedom and independence to do as they please even if it causes inequity for children, OR I limit faculty and staff freedom, love them a little less, and remind them that they are not self-employed, they work for the school district, and they are first and foremost required to do what's best for the students, even at their own peril. At all times, even if it does make life tougher for the faculty, we exist to serve and pay attention to our students. Be professional! Love the students. Students' needs first. Faculty and staff's needs second.

Isn't it possible that as a school leader you can pay attention to, benefit from, and invest emotionally in *both* the adults and the students?

Appreciating the importance of being committed to both adults and students was a difficult lesson for me to learn at the outset of my PLC leadership work. When I began as a PLC leader, I was struck by how far the pendulum had swung on the side of "doing what was best for the adults." It seemed that very few of our decisions were based on what would be best for the students or their parents. Many inequities in student learning were obvious, but it didn't seem to matter as long as teachers could do the job their own way. Students were often inconvenienced because the faculty and staff chose not to look at life from the student point of view.

Our faculty at Stevenson valued personal independence—it was faster and quicker to get things done if we did not need to be interdependent. Yet we knew students would benefit if the adults worked together to ensure equitable learning experiences across grades or courses. Such conditions required a deeper and more engaged experience with colleagues but intruded on personal time and energy.

Some of our faculty valued getting lessons developed quickly and often at the last minute—for them, it was easier not to work with others. Yet we knew students would benefit from the adult discussions around well-designed lessons. Some of our faculty valued returning tests and assessments only when they could find time for grading. Urgency and priority were not considered. Yet we knew our students would benefit from immediate and corrective feedback on assessments, as well as the subsequent faculty assessment discussions around common assessments. Such activity was more time-consuming for the faculty, some of whom perceived it as not what was best for the adults. Some of our faculty valued designing and reusing their own "stuff." Yet we knew our students would benefit when that stuff was shared across grade levels or courses and revised as part of a formative learning process. Some of our faculty valued personal experience about what works and doesn't work in the classroom. Yet we knew our students would benefit from the certainty and practice of research-affirmed instruction aimed at improved student learning. The research discussions were slated to become part of the work of the PLC learning teams, and, again, more time was required for deeper discussion.

In some ways, as you begin to push hard on creating a viable PLC culture, the pendulum begins to shift away from what is best and most convenient for the adults to what is best and most convenient for the students. Figure 4.1 illustrates the tension that arises as you transition from pre-PLC culture to a fully engaged PLC culture.

In a fully engaged PLC, all aspects of the vision begin to focus appropriately on what the adults will do to ensure all students learn well. However, as the pendulum swings toward the perspective of the student and student achievement, if you are not careful, the adults can lose their sense of value and importance.

As we began our PLC pursuit, our pendulum was so far toward doing what was best for the adults that we were not benefitting the students. As a leader, I pushed extremely hard to swing the pendulum to the other side. I demanded that we do what was best for students, that we view our work through the lens of student learning, and that all of our decisions become based on what we understood through that lens. Along the way, however, I lost some of the faculty and staff, because I forgot to invest the same amount of leadership time and energy into *them*. And as with any pendulum, the answer does not lie at the extremes. It lies in the middle. As leaders, we have to make decisions that love the students *and* love the faculty.

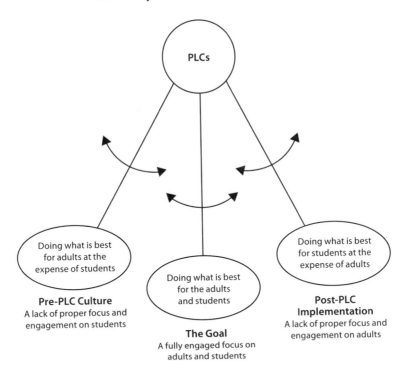

**Figure 4.1: The pendulum of PLC leadership focus and engagement.**

*Visit **go.solution-tree.com/plcbooks** to download a reproducible version of this figure.*

Midway though my PLC leadership life, I had to adjust my thinking to focus on these questions:

> *How do I mobilize the faculty to work interdependently, to do what is best for students—even at their own personal sacrifice sometimes? And how do I provide the support, communication, care, and understanding the adults need to feel valued, loved, emotionally important, and well treated?*

Fullan's (2008) notion that no stakeholder is more important than any other must not be lost on the PLC leader. It's not *just* about the students. In fact, it's really all about student learning and growth *and* adult learning and growth, intricately woven together, forever:

> The fundamental emerging leadership belief themes indicate leaders in learning organization school cultures do what is best for supporting adults and adult learning. At the same time, the focused intent and purpose of the adult learning is to do what is best for student learning and improving student experiences and achievement. (Kanold, 2002, p. 187)

Balanced leadership is about creating and sustaining a great place for students *and* adults to learn and grow.

Paying attention to the adults *and* the students requires emotional commitment and engagement on your part. In turn, emotional attachment and deep relationships require energy. As a leader, investing yourself in the faculty and staff *in relation to the high-quality purpose and vision of success for every student* is the bedrock of your evidence for success. When your energy is low, it impedes your ability to focus on deep relationships with others. You start to take for granted those closest to you, those in your sphere of influence. Ultimately you and those around you miss out on one of the primary benefits of the professional learning community—a fully engaged work life. If you don't monitor your energy levels and pace yourself, you and your teams will find yourselves living in the world of PLC-lite: unable to do the real work of learning community adults, unable to reap the real benefits for students.

# Providing Motivation 3.0

A fundamental benefit of effective professional learning community cultures is the full engagement of every adult stakeholder every day. PLCs, when led well, provide the catalyst for a more engaged and motivated workforce. The mark of a highly successful PLC leader is the creation of a school culture maintained by highly engaged adults who are committed to the right set of expected behaviors and lifelong learning.

A report by the National Center for Analysis of Longitudinal Data in Educational Research (King Rice, 2010) sheds light on the critical importance of getting school leadership right. The studies reviewed in this report provide evidence that the quality of engagement by the school leaders—including the principal—affect teachers' satisfaction and their decisions about where to work, parents' perceptions about the schools their children attend, and ultimately, the academic performance of the school.

You are making progress in your PLC leadership journey if you are living a more fully engaged, autonomous, and intrinsically motivated work life, and if you are creating the conditions that allow those in your N-S-E-W sphere to have the same experience. One of the more remarkable benefits to your PLC leadership influence is increased stakeholder engagement in and commitment to critical actions necessary to teach and lead children well, not because of any external rewards, but because of the improved personal satisfaction they receive from their work.

Yet when left to their own devices, without the right motivation, many educational stakeholders (faculty and administrators) are likely to *not* fully engage in their work life. Sometimes we assume that because people have chosen educating children as their profession, they are intrinsically more responsible—that they will consistently hold themselves accountable for giving their full engagement, energy, and motivation; work to attain the mastery of knowledge necessary to lead students; and do so with appropriate amounts of energy and preparation every day. Who will you be as a professional when no one is looking? Inadequate self-monitoring of your energy levels will result in a drift away from sustained engagement, motivation, and enjoyment.

How do leaders monitor the engagement of others? Pink (2009) explains that the more traditional "Motivation 2.0" leadership sought compliance to the necessary work of the school. In pre-PLC school culture, personal motivation often depends on a system of external rewards determined by others. In our district, for example, there was a tendency to shift responsibility for personal morale and motivation onto those to our north—the tier 3 level of accountability. Pink points out the limitations of vertical accountability as an effective tool for helping those in your sphere of influence to pursue a sustained "desire to get better and better at something that matters"; as he notes, "Motivation 2.0's goal [is] to encourage people to do things in a particular ways—that is to get them to comply" (p. 111). Compliance is not the preferred way of the successful PLC leader.

PLC cultures are more in line with what Pink refers to as the next generation: Motivation 3.0, which seeks engagement that produces the desire for and the pursuit of "what really matters" (p. 111). To achieve this engagement requires your willingness to steward your own energy level, as well as that of the organization. Otherwise, the system drags. Think about it. Identify those adults in your N-S-E-W sphere of influence. How many, at this moment, are feeding energy into and around things that really matter at a high level? How many are creating an organizational drag due to their own willingness to mismanage their energy and their work engagement, *because they can?* Loehr and Schwartz (2003) further state it like this:

> They [leaders] inspire or demoralize others first by how effectively they manage their own energy and next by how well they mobilize, focus, invest and renew the collective energy for those they lead. The skillful management of energy, individually and organizationally, makes possible something that we call full engagement. (p. 5)

There is a reason that many adults in a school organization can come to school and not be fully engaged in a high- and positive-energy work life every day. First, they openly choose *not* to strategically engage, and they disengage from high-energy activities and from the general community. The consequences of only giving 50 to 75 percent to the job, or coming to school angry, resentful, and exhausted, are, more likely than not, *nothing*.

In education, consequences for a "less-than-full engagement" day by the teacher or school leader are rarely profound. "I'm exhausted, and I don't feel like giving it my best today" has significantly different consequences for a cardiac surgeon than for an educator. Nonetheless, disengaged teachers and leaders do place students' lives at risk. It's just a more invisible long-term effect that is often measured too late. Although PLC cultures can create conditions that ultimately help to achieve a more fully engaged workforce, the result is difficult to achieve without tremendous organizational energy that aspires to high levels of lateral and self-accountability to the work.

As Pink (2009) indicates, the most notable feature of the modern workplace may be its lack of engagement and its disregard for mastery: the things that really matter! He cites 2009 Gallup research that indicates "in the United States, more than 50 percent of employees are not engaged at work—and nearly 20 percent are actively disengaged" (p. 111). In our profession, faculty, staff, and administration are for the most part allowed to choose their level of engagement in their work. If the Gallup poll statistics hold true for all professions, imagine the challenge of trying to motivate a faculty and staff when 20 percent or more are actively disengaged from their daily work of teaching and leading, and a possible 50 percent may not be working to their full potential.

In the end, Motivation 2.0, or PLCs by compliance, is neither the goal nor the solution to the motivation dilemma. Motivation 3.0 is the answer and what really matters. This is where you as a school leader and those you lead begin training to meet the PLC expectations of defined autonomy, to enjoy an engaged work life with others, and to experience and grow from optimal adult learning experiences in your teams.

The question becomes, how do you, as a leader, continuously monitor the energy of your life so that you will be able to become a Motivation 3.0 leader? PLC leadership is as much about the process and the culture of relational energy you nurture as it is about the product or results you help to produce and sustain. You improve the leadership energy of those in your sphere of influence when you sustain the pursuit of optimal work experiences.

# Pursuing Optimal Learning Experiences

PLC leaders pursue the tenets Peter Senge (1990) established as the core elements of the work of learning organizations in *The Fifth Discipline: The Art & Practice of the Learning Organization*. At the time, Senge was concerned the organizational theory described in the book would become a fad. However, more than twenty years later, *The Fifth Discipline*, revised in 2006, continues to provide the solid foundation for and fundamental insight into our work as professional learning community leaders.

At the same time the *Fifth Discipline* was released, psychologist Mihaly Csikszentmihalyi (pronounced CHICK-sent-me-hi) summarized his fifteen-year study regarding the experience of peak-performing work life in his book *Flow: The Classic Work on How to Achieve Happiness* (2002). The impact of his work has also been sustained for more than twenty years, including an updated version in 2008. Csikszentmihalyi (2008) is the leading researcher and architect of the notion of what he called *flow*: "the way people describe their state of mind when consciousness is harmoniously ordered, and they want to pursue whatever they are doing for its own sake" (p. 6). As a PLC leader, you are in the state of flow when your focus is energized, your involvement is deep, and your engagement is total. This context contributes to experiencing incredible success in the process of activities conducted over days, weeks, or months. Senge's *Fifth Discipline* helped clarify the work-related pursuits of professional learning communities, and Csikszentmihalyi's *Flow* helped clarify both the hope and the meaning professional learning community cultures would bring to our leadership work and life experiences.

For the professional learning community leader, these two theories merge around the development of effective learning teams. Is it possible for you and your leadership teams to create optimal learning experiences and be "in the flow" at work, fully energized, and fully engaged? The answer is yes. Flow is a fully engaged high-energy state that has meaning and internal purpose for the faculty as members of learning teams. Your PLC leadership involves training yourself to experience life flow and to help your teams to experience the same. In many cases this will require you to create working conditions and opportunities that will move the teams into flow at the same time they are struggling to maintain optimal energy to meet the new demands of the PLC culture. When you are in the flow of your work life, you as an individual, or you as part of a team, begin to take on more complex challenges without feeling overwhelmed. Csikszentmihalyi (2008) states it like this: "It [flow activities] provided a sense of discovery, a creative feeling of transporting the person to higher levels of performance, and led to previously undreamed of states of consciousness" (p. 266).

Csikszentmihalyi (2008) presents a graphic that helps highlight the two dimensions of flow: your level of skill and knowledge versus your level of current tasks and challenges. Figure 4.2 is an adaptation and representation of these aspects of the flow model for PLC learning teams.

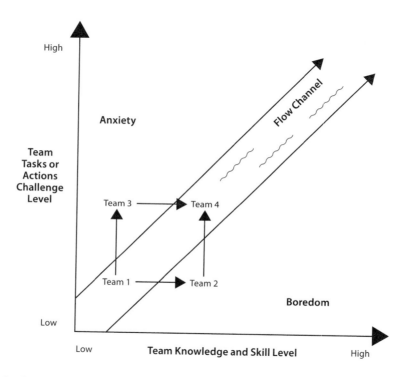

**Figure 4.2: Professional learning community flow.**

*Source: Figure (adapted) page 74, from FLOW: THE PSYCHOLOGY OF OPTIMAL EXPERIENCE by MIHALY CSIKSZENTMIHALYI. Copyright © 1990 by Mihaly Csikszentmihalyi. Reprinted by permission of HarperCollins Publishers.*

*Visit go.solution-tree.com/plcbooks to download a reproducible version of this figure.*

The concept of flow provides excellent guidance for your own leadership actions as well as the actions and task selection of your PLC learning teams. To keep your teams at a level of optimal performance, you must achieve the proper balance between their current knowledge and skill level and the level of complexity for the new task actions or challenges. Figure 4.2 shows four teams, each in a different state of flow. Team 1 is in the flow channel but not at a very complex level of work—low skills and low tasks. As indicated by the arrow, Team 1 will drift to *boredom* if the level of task demand stays too low, or shift into *anxiety* if workload expectations increase before the team has developed the proper knowledge and capacity. Keeping teams in the flow requires reflection and balance.

One of the more positive aspects of effective team learning and sharing is the ongoing nature of knowledge and skill development during team meetings and team learning time. The professional development and growth that take place as a result of the PLC workplace should allow the team to *increase* its level of task challenges. Under the right conditions, the increasing complexity of ongoing work-related tasks of the PLC team should coincide with its growing knowledge and skill development; this is necessary in order to stay out of the range of Team 2 in figure 4.2—a place of boredom and disengagement. For Team 2, the task challenge is so weak the team becomes bored and loses its purpose. Team members will ask, "Why does our team need to meet?" To help Team 2 move back into the flow channel, your job as a PLC leader is to increase the task expectations for the team. As the level, quality, and depth of the work become more complex and more meaningful, Team 2 will move toward the flow channel.

This is exactly the goal of a professional learning community—as the knowledge and skills of the learning team increases, the ability of the adults to impact student achievement at a more complex level increases. Eventually, the school organization as a system gets into the flow channel, able to create and take action toward more complex tasks. Over time, as teams are able to develop capacity and take on more tasks, movement along the flow channel will reflect more complex task activity by the team.

If the challenge is so great the team collapses from the stress of the task, however, the team (as well as individuals) will fall out of the flow channel. The extent to which you can stretch and challenge each team toward optimal flow activities varies widely, based on the current knowledge or skill capacity of the team. To move Team 3 to flow, for example, requires ongoing skill and knowledge capacity development. It is the only way to keep this team fully engaged in its work. It is important to note that the leadership response for Team 3 would *not* be to significantly lower the task expectations down to the level of Team 1. Team 1 might be in the flow channel, but operating at such a low level of complexity that it will not meet your PLC task expectations. In other words, the team members might be having an enjoyable experience, but they're not really accomplishing much. Full engagement in flow means to stretch forward to new levels of complexity in the channel.

Csikszentmihalyi (2008) points out an incredibly important PLC leadership lesson at this point. In figure 4.2, although Team 4 is shown in the flow channel, it "does not represent a stable situation" (p. 266). Although Team 4 might be in a more complex and enjoyable energy state at the moment, the team will wander in and out of the channel. It will either become bored by the current level of tasks and challenge expectations, or become frustrated by its inability to perform new task challenges. The latter is often an issue when the task expectations stay the same from one year to the next, even though the members of the team are new to the team, grade level, or course. Any shift in the dynamics of the skill or knowledge level of the team can move the team out of the flow channel.

Measure the placement of your current teams on the flow diagram provided in figure 4.2. Your teams will exist in a variety of places within or outside of the flow channel. One of your tasks as a PLC leader is to create opportunities for the teams to either stay in or move toward the flow channel—and then to keep the teams moving "up" the flow channel to more complex levels of work performance. This effort requires constantly striving for improvement by the teachers, the teacher teams, and the students. On occasion, you may be required to move a team out of the flow channel by introducing new task challenges that temporarily cause the team some disquiet and discomfort as members develop new knowledge and skills. The same is true for you. As a PLC leader, you must also monitor and manage the flow of your own tasks and activities and be very careful to notice when either boredom or stress negatively affects the energy of your leadership life.

Are you personally improving your level of complexity up the flow channel while remaining fully engaged in your work? Do you use specific strategies to help you stay in the flow channel in your leadership work? The following five flow strategies will help you and your teams move toward and along the flow channel of your work experience.

1. **Establish clear goals.** Are expectations and goals attainable? Do they align appropriately with the skill set and abilities of the team? Are the levels of task challenge and knowledge and skills low or high for the team and team leader?

2. **Limit the number of goals.** Is there a high degree of team concentration on a limited number of tasks? Will the team engaged in the

task have the opportunity to focus on the task action and delve deeply into it throughout the year?

3. **Provide direct and immediate feedback.** How will the team receive feedback on what is and is not working—successes and failures—during the course of implementing the required tasks? Does the team have a formative way to adjust its work on the task actions throughout the school year?

4. **Monitor for balance.** How will the team leader measure the team's ability or knowledge and skill level against the challenge level of the task? Are the assigned tasks neither too easy nor too difficult? This factor must be monitored throughout the school year. There should be some stretch and discomfort as the team grows into the task. How will this factor be monitored?

5. **Support autonomy.** Does the team have a sense of personal control over how to perform the task or activity? The activity must become intrinsically rewarding to inspire effortless action by the team—otherwise it becomes a burden.

(Visit **go.solution-tree.com/plcbooks** to download the worksheet *Five Strategies for Movement Toward and Along the Flow Channel*.)

PLC leaders should seek the benefits of positive leadership energy experienced in flow. By using the five flow strategies, you and your leadership team can train to get better at living in a state of flow characterized by high energy and engagement. Ultimately, it is important to realize that staying in the flow requires working very hard to reach new levels of competency and complexity on the knowledge and skills you, as well as each team member, need to master. In a PLC, it may take time before the results of the hard work are in evidence. As Pink (2009) reminds us, "It is grueling to be sure. But that is not the problem, that's the solution" (p. 125).

Your optimal leadership performance occurs when your energy is both high and positive. You, and all those in your N-S-E-W sphere, live for the experience of a work life that is in the flow, a work life that provides continuous growth and renewal. When working in the flow, you tend to lead well, moving beyond the superficial task completion into the deeper and more satisfying relationship development and professional inquiry necessary for effective PLC leadership. When living in the flow, you are more helpful, hopeful, joyful, confident, and connected to others. Such are the attributes of highly effective PLC leaders. Those you lead, whether students or adults, need you to be in the flow at work—all the time, every day.

And yet, too much time spent working at high-energy and high-level activities can leave you ineffective as a PLC leader. Take a moment to reflect on the definition of the discipline of reflection and balance:

**The leadership work of intentionally and strategically engaging in and disengaging from high-energy activities**

Your survival as a fully engaged, high-energy-level, "in the flow" PLC leader is dependent upon your ability to strategically and intentionally plan for disengagement from high-energy activities. Train yourself to ensure that you lead a reflective and balanced existence in both your work and personal lives.

# Becoming Engaged and Reflective

In *The Power of Full Engagement*, Loehr and Schwartz (2003) explain, "The challenge of great performance is to manage your energy more effectively in all dimensions to achieve your goals" (p. 9). These authors highlight the distinction between managing your time and managing your energy when they state, "The numbers of hours in a day are fixed, but the quantity and quality of energy is not" (p. 4).

One of the more helpful diagrams in their book highlights the dynamics of energy based on two criteria: (1) negative to positive emotional energy (the horizontal axis), compared against (2) low to high physical energy (the vertical axis). As discussed earlier in this chapter, effective PLC leaders are aware of and protective of their personal energy levels and the traps that cause energy to be drained or gained throughout the day, week, month, and school year. This energy grid (Loehr & Schwartz, 2003, p. 10) has been adapted in figure 4.3 to our purposes for PLC leadership. The energy grid places more of an emphasis on the discipline of energy management and monitoring (a more variant option) and less on the time available to do your leadership tasks (a more fixed option). The energy grid is defined by four distinct quadrants:

- **Quadrant I–High positive energy.** This quadrant represents the full engagement and "in the flow" place of your work life. It is where all those who work with you expect you to exist each day.

- **Quadrant II–Low positive energy.** This is the quadrant where you must spend some leadership time every day, week, month, and year, or you will never sustain a Quadrant I state of flow in your work life.

- **Quadrant III—High negative energy.** Living in this quadrant makes you very unpleasant to work with, drags down those in your N-S-E-W spheres, and makes it very difficult to achieve a state of flow.

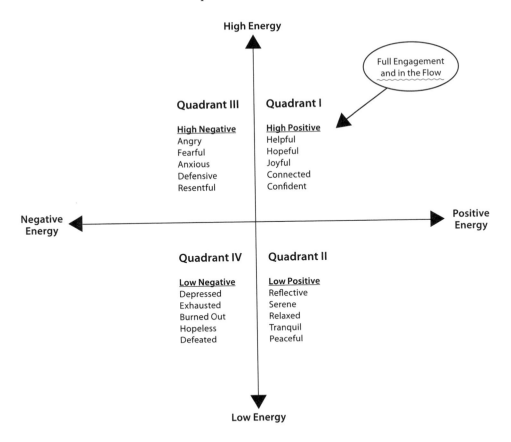

**Figure 4.3: The PLC energy quadrants.**

- **Quadrant IV—Low negative energy.** In this quadrant, it's very difficult for you to function as a leader, teacher, or team member. It very difficult to transition out of this quadrant without help and support.

## Quadrant I: Optimal Experiences

The energy grid described in figure 4.3 provides an image that can sum up your PLC leadership life pursuit in nine words: *live life daily in Quadrant I and Quadrant II.* The overall goal is to become a PLC leader who experiences flow—a Quadrant I work life. It is in Quadrant I that you become fully engaged and more personally satisfied. It is in Quadrant I that you are most likely to create the work experiences that lead to flow. In this quadrant, you experience optimal performance: your energy is high and positive. When those in your N-S-E-W sphere are also in Quadrant I, you will rarely need to use tier 3 compliance as a motivational tool for the vision and values. Daniel Pink's (2009) Motivation 3.0 reigns supreme here. The well-trained PLC leader passionately pursues the Quadrant I high-positive-energy life and seeks to create conditions that support the same pursuit from others. As Loehr and Schwartz assert, "Full engagement and maximum performance are possible only in the high positive quadrant" (2003, p. 10).

When working and living in Quadrant I, you are more likely to lead others (students and adults) toward a Quadrant I life at work—all the time, every day. When you are in Quadrant I, all of the speed issues dissipate. Technology? Great tool, and it helps you to be more efficient. It *feeds* your energy, and you have its interruption potential under control. Faulty assumptions? These vanish; there is no need for making excuses. Victim speak and laying blame disappear. Superficiality? Not a chance. Overwhelmed by your workload? Not a chance of that, either— you are in the flow! Quadrant I leaders are *connected* to others and aware of how their leadership actions and inactions affect others. Inability to value both adults *and* students simultaneously? No again. Servant leadership soars. Quadrant I is a great place to be. A high-positive, fully engaged, fully energized work life—a super PLC leader's life.

There is one major problem, however. Too much time in Quadrant I—186 days or so in a typical school year—will drive you and others into Quadrants III and IV pretty fast. School leaders and learning teams who drift toward day-to-day work within Quadrants III and IV will devastate the culture of the school and the programs they serve. You, the learning teams, and the programs you lead must avoid Quadrants III and IV at all costs—for yourself, for your colleagues, and for the sake of your school and your family.

## *Quadrants III and IV: Negative Experiences*

The goal for your leadership life, then, is to manage the energy and habits of your day so as to avoid Quadrants III and IV. The bad news is that you will naturally drift toward anger, fear, impatience, defensiveness, resentment, and exhaustion. If these negative factors are left unchecked, you will inadvertently drift toward Quadrants III and IV. And as you do so, you become less and less effective as a PLC leader. How do you avoid this drift? How do you avoid the high negative energy of Quadrant III? First, you discipline yourself to routinely examine and monitor awareness of your leadership energy. To begin your monitoring, reflect on these eight symptoms of drifting toward Quadrants III and IV:

1. You have a chronic sense that there is never enough time to get your job done.

2. You complete other people's sentences.

3. You answer the phone with "What do you want, I'm busy!" or "What's up?" [suggesting, "You're bothering me"]

4. You are running late throughout the day.

5. You feel tired throughout the day.

6. You forget significant events in the lives of those closest to you.

7. You feel constant physical tension in your neck, shoulders, arms, and legs.

8. You constantly complain to your friends about how busy you are.

If four of the eight symptoms are often true for you, then your drift away from optimal work experiences has already begun. Being in either Quadrant III (high negative boorish leadership energy and behavior) or Quadrant IV (low negative disengaged leadership energy behaviors) makes it *impossible* for you to lead and sustain a constructive PLC environment. With few exceptions, tolerance for Quadrant III behavior must be very *low* in the horizontal and vertical accountability systems throughout the professional learning community.

In 2006, I presented the idea of "living a Quadrant I and II life" to the faculty and staff in our consortium of school districts. It seemed to me that a crystal-clear understanding and self-analysis of the current "energy state" of our school organization would begin with each individual adult sitting in the room. As I presented and explained the four energy quadrant descriptors, I asked for a show of hands (there were about 1,100 people in the room) from anyone who worked with someone who was currently demonstrating Quadrant III or IV behavior (interestingly, all of those "someones" were sitting in the room as well). More than two thirds of the hands were raised.

I was not surprised. It was early March. We had been at the frantic pace of leading and teaching for seven months, and the work takes its toll. The idea of monitoring our energy levels—paying attention to our level of engagement and support for our collaborative work—was not something we had publicly addressed before. For several months after that day, I would hear people say to each other, "Oh no, don't go there. You're drifting into Quadrant III behavior! Get back here!"

So, how do PLC leaders and those in their N-S-E-W sphere avoid the inevitable drift out of Quadrant I and into Quadrants III and IV?

## *Quadrant II: Renewal Experiences*

Although you live for the experience of a Quadrant I life, too much time in either Quadrant I or Quadrant III will send you deep into Quadrant IV. In other words, you must discipline yourself to *strategically disengage* from Quadrant I and simultaneously engage in meaningful Quadrant II—positive emotional, low physical energy—time. This "downtime" allows you to regather, recoup, renew, and refresh.

How much time is needed in the reflective time of Quadrant II is dependent on the individual. Individuals have their own "enough-is-enough" line where the undesired energy path to Quadrant III and IV begins. Your line that crosses over into Quadrant III behavior may or may not be the same as that of the leader working next to you. Over the years I have worked with colleagues who crossed the line very quickly and needed to be diligent about balancing their time in Quadrant I with time in Quadrant II *daily*. Other leaders could seemingly go weeks at a time without any signs of drift, somehow maintaining high energy levels every day at work as long as they reached out for Quadrant II time once or twice a month.

A real danger is that if you leave the drift unchecked, it will take you a bit longer to get back to Quadrant I. As a leader, you must know yourself well enough to know when fully engaged and active becomes hurried and dispassionate. Use the eight symptoms of drift to gauge when enough is enough. You can also seek out trusted friends or colleagues and ask them to be crystal clear when they see you start to drift. They will recognize the signs long before you do. The question is, are you willing to hear them?

Interestingly, superficial learning teams often have a collective negative or low energy that enables participants to drift into Quadrant III, and sometimes Quadrant IV, behavior. In those cases, team members will tolerate and ignore behaviors and verbal messages that are toxic to effective PLC growth and development.

Effective PLC team members and leaders discipline themselves to notice when colleagues are drifting out of Quadrant I. They provide the necessary support, encouragement, and tough love that prevent colleagues from drifting into Quadrant III and Quadrant IV. They take care of one another. When observing a colleague being angry and resentful with a student or parent, PLC colleagues take the time to find out *why* that person is exhibiting Quadrant III behavior—and then they take the time and the energy necessary to talk with that colleague about the Quadrant III behavior.

The Discipline of Reflection and Balance    147

Wise and well-disciplined PLC leaders know this: if you do not practice to get better at *strategic disengagement* from Quadrant I, you will eventually end up bitter, frustrated, and ineffective. Leaders who balance time between Quadrant I and Quadrant II generally avoid the malady of job fatigue: low energy, disengagement from work, and superficial leadership.

# Creating Balance

I consistently hear complaints from colleagues, parents, friends, and family about how difficult it is to live a balanced life. I cannot remember a year when the issue of balance wasn't a concern—either major or minor—for administrators, faculty, parents, and students. If you asked most educators and school leaders what they most seek, they would probably say something related to a balanced lifestyle and the requisite time to get it all done.

We live in an era when students and adults are bound by a fast-paced life, driven by their schedules, planners, text messages, cell phones, computers, and smartphones. The demands of our schedules eat into the very essence of our existence. So what we most seek is a balanced life—time for work, play, family, friends, travel, academic study, hobbies, reflection, and sleep. We want Quadrant I *and* Quadrant II time. This is our quest.

And yet, in our pursuit of balance and the Quadrant I and II life, we tend to act as victims, as if we are running harder, training faster, and spending more time in Quadrant I because of the demands of others rather than the demands we have placed on ourselves. *"A slow sort of country," said the Queen. "Now, here, you see, it takes all the running you can do, to stay in the same place. If you want to get somewhere else, you must run at least twice as fast as that!"* The Red Queen of speed controls us, we claim, not the other way around.

PLC leaders often act as if they are not in control of whether or not they can live a balanced life. The discipline to train for deep reflection demands you become intentional about strategically finding your Quadrant II time—regardless of the pace of your days. Of course, when you are really busy, training for quiet Quadrant II time is the first thing that you stop doing. Just like training to get back in shape, discipline in the gym is often the last thing you squeeze in, and then you are just too tired to go after all. You must choose to discipline yourself for quiet, low-energy reflection time, and you must not let that time get squeezed out of an already full day.

School leaders, especially PLC school leaders, just don't know how to slow down. You don't want to slow down. You don't have time to slow down. But as I have already mentioned, this is *not a time* issue. Slowing down is an energy issue. The question isn't when you will find the time to engage in the low-energy moments of Quadrant II. The question is, *What must you do to ensure you have the energy required for full engagement in your leadership life?* How do you spend *and* recover the energy you need? The well-disciplined PLC leader understands that Quadrant II reflective time is *not* optional, even though it may be unattractive, uninteresting, and the last thing you really want to do.

Take another look at figure 4.3 (page 143). Quadrant II is low-positive-energy time for a leader. During Quadrant II time, you are serene, reflective, relaxed, tranquil, and peaceful. It is a time during which you purposely plan silence into your life. No music, no TV. And for almost every leader I know, it is usually an uncomfortable experience, at least in the beginning. You are so used to noise, to doing stuff, to staying busy. You generally are not accustomed to silence. My personal idea of slowing down was to play softball or basketball three to five nights after work. It was my way of balancing the stress of work. The only problem was that it too required full-engaged Quadrant I energy to play. There was no time to renew. I needed to practice slowing my pace more intentionally, but it wasn't easy.

Csikszentmihalyi (2008) reminds us, "The best moments of our lives are not the passive receptive, relaxing times—although such experiences can be enjoyable, if we have worked hard to attain them" (p. 24). It is true that the best moments are those fully engaged around complex tasks—peak Quadrant I experiences. PLC leaders—like you—thrive on those moments. I thrived on those moments. But those moments cannot be sustained without intentional disengagement to avoid eventual burnout. You can choose to ignore the effects of no exercise, but eventually lack of exercise will take its toll on you physically. Likewise, you can choose to ignore the effects of no Quadrant II time, but eventually lack of reflection will render you ineffective as a PLC leader.

Solitude is what is required for Quadrant II, and solitude allows for introspection on your work. This introspection can also be achieved through a deep friendship that allows for an honest accounting and intimate discussion of how things are really going in your leadership world. In 2002, when I became superintendent, my administrative assistant noticed I often scheduled a gentleman named John Tunis into my weekly planner, usually for an hour of time. After a few months in which John failed to show up, she asked me why he kept missing his appointment. I replied it was probably because, as a favorite childhood author of mine, he had died many years before. What I was actually doing was scheduling a Quadrant II, low-positive-energy moment in my intense workday. This time for reflection and intermittent disengagement helped me to evaluate current progress and re-engage for the next activities of the day. I was fiercely protective of this time for reflection within the madness of the day's work.

There are, of course, other daily actions you can take to slow down for some low-energy, meaningful, and reflective Quadrant II time. Such actions include the following:

- During the week, plan windows of time with nothing on your schedule except reflective brainstorming or work on your six-by-six list (see page 124).

- Purposely stand in a longer line at the store, and do not look at your PDA or cell phone.

- Take off your watch and shut down your email on the weekends. Leave an emergency contact number if needed.

- Plan time to deliberately wait for someone—show up early—and while waiting, give yourself permission to do nothing but notice your surroundings.

- Stop texting, blogging, or emailing for planned periods of time each day and each week.

Most importantly, however, find brief periods of time for solitude and reflection: no inputs, no noise, no other voices from colleagues, family, or friends coming at you (unless invited). Solitude comes in many forms for leaders. Some like the quiet stillness of the early morning. Others like to run or jog or walk. Others prefer to write in a journal or to just let their minds decompress as they do household chores. The key is that whatever you do to quiet your mind, do it in real solitude: just you, your thoughts, and low energy. Use solitude as an opportunity to become aware of your own personal attitudes, mindsets, and beliefs. Use it as a chance to learn more about yourself as you renew your Quadrant I commitments to your leadership work and world.

Use your time in solitude to reflect on your work and your work life. Simply ask yourself, How am I doing? Who did I forget to notice today? What do I need to focus on in the next six weeks? What are my priorities? Am I spending quality time with my family? What did I learn from that crisis today? How will/should

I respond differently next time? How can I make this vision action more clear to everyone? Am I treating everyone with respect and appreciation? Am I willing to at least listen to others' perspectives even if I disagree with them? Which of my teams are out of the flow channel? The list is endless. Quality reflection time is not about reflecting on what others need to do better. It is about reflecting on what *you* need to do, and who you need to become, in order to bring the correct energy, mindset, and problem-solving skills to a better "next time" at your school.

You spend time reflecting on the past to impact a better future. You examine how well you are engaging others in difficult decisions without being condescending or judgmental. You examine areas of your school leadership that are working at a superficial level. You decide how to best take a plan of action to stop the trend to get things done in a hurry. For some leaders, this is best achieved through deep conversations with a trusted other. Regardless of how you approach your time for reflection (alone or with someone), Quadrant II time is *required* for your personal growth, energy management, and internal balance.

# Pursuing Internal Balance

Ultimately, training strictly for a leadership life that balances a lot of activities is an inadequate goal. If your fundamental goal as a PLC leader is to seek external balance for all of the things you need to do, then you will have aimed too low. The pursuit of external balance alone causes you to pursue mediocrity and often results in too many leadership tasks performed at an average level. And as indicated previously, you will position yourself as a victim: "It's someone else's fault I don't pursue the discipline of balance. *They* ask too much of me." External balance is not the "one thing" that leads to more effective PLC leadership life. Continuously training for *internal balance* is the mark of effective PLC leaders.

In the movie *City Slickers*, Billy Crystal plays a forty-year-old in the grips of a midlife crisis who participates in a "vacation" cattle drive with two of his boyhood pals. During the cattle drive, the lead ranch hand, Curly (played by Jack Palance), tells Crystal there is one thing that is the secret to life. After several days and nights on the trail, Curly finally indicates he will reveal the one thing the next morning. The next day, Crystal wakes up only to find Curly in a frozen pose, holding up one finger, having died while on watch the night before. Caught in his midlife crisis, Crystal still didn't know the one thing that should be the target of his quest for an ideal life (Crystal, Smith, & Underwood, 1991).

By the end of the movie, Crystal realizes that at a deeper level, the pursuit of external balance didn't capture his sense of compelling urgency for a life worthy of human devotion. If Curly would have revealed the one thing, I suspect it would have been the paradigm that life is to be given to something bigger than one's self. This perspective is a critical aspect of a PLC leader's thinking. Do you want to give yourself to a school cause that is greater than you? Do you want to help your PLC learning teams to collaborate and create a culture of learning that is far greater than any one of them could produce alone? George Bernard Shaw (1903) captured this notion in his preface to *Man and Superman:*

> This is the true joy in life, the being used for a purpose recognized by yourself as mighty one; the being thoroughly worn out before you are thrown on the scrap heap; the being a force of nature instead of a feverish selfish little clod of ailments and grievances complaining the world will not devote itself to making you happy. (p. 32)

You can be a force of nature, influencing your leadership world with the power of Quadrant I energy, or you can be a complaining, selfish victim of your leadership circumstances—a Quadrant III toxic leader.

The pursuit of external balance as *the* goal assumes your problems are beyond your control. *The world will not devote itself to making you happy.* If you wait for outside circumstances to change, you fall prey to the plague of *if onlys.* If only the Internet didn't exist (eliminating blogs, email, Twitter, Facebook, and parent portals); if only the board of education, the community, and the faculty didn't have such high expectations; if only the local press would just leave you alone; if only your teacher teams would be more fully functioning on their own; if only the parents would just stop complaining and be more helpful . . . then, you think, you could lead a more balanced work life. *Not so.*

At home you think, if only the holiday season wasn't so demanding; if only you didn't have to drive to and from work in dense traffic; if only your children weren't in so many activities; if only the dog wouldn't shed; if only your relatives were all healthy . . . then you could lead a more balanced personal life. *Not so.*

The answer lies not in eliminating external disorder, but in seeking out the reflective Quadrant II time that will help you to face the *internal* disorder of your life. It lies in creating the internal order that allows you to do a few things really, really well—and to do them at a deep and meaningful level.

This is why continued training to become a reflective practitioner is a required part of the development for the PLC leadership discipline of reflection and balance. The effective PLC leader takes time every day, week, month, and year to perform internal checks. Does my behavior reflect positive character, good intentions, and rock-solid values? Are my intentions and interactions honest, sans hidden intentions? Is my voice to others authentic and sincere? Do others trust what I say, and can they hear *how* I say it? Am I making internal and mature decisions not to live an unbalanced, out-of-flow life? Do I know myself well enough to notice my drift into Quadrants III and IV? Do I understand that what is balance and reflection time for me may not be the same for others? I may or may not be able to keep the same pace as others, and vice versa. Maybe I can handle the demands of leading another task force. Maybe I like to journal to collect my thoughts. Another colleague may not be able to meet the demands of a new task force right now due to constraints of family or other related duties. To relax and reflect, he might not like to journal—but perhaps I've come across him calmly eating ice cream in the quiet of his parked car. Quadrant II time is an experience unique to each PLC leader.

You become a superficial PLC leader the moment you stop paying attention to the balance and quality of life for each individual in your N-S-E-W sphere. Yes, you must care and notice. And if you do care, you cannot try a one-size-fits-all approach to providing support. Authentic PLC leaders make balance and reflection a priority and get the point that it might look and feel different to different leaders and members of the PLC. They insist, however, that each member of the PLC finds the internal balance he or she needs so that excellence and a high-energy work life can become the norm.

When you strive to seek a balanced leadership life, you develop the internal discipline to say no, to adjust other commitments and life goals as new passions and pursuits take root. As you become a model of internal balance for your colleagues, you help them learn how to live in Quadrant I energy at work, while becoming intentional about taking Quadrant II low-energy time for reflection and rest. The stakes are high. The leader's failure to create a culture of reflection and internal balance will leave too many members of the PLC stranded in Quadrants III and IV. They will be ineffective in their jobs, they will be difficult to be around, they will be toxic to the improvement of the school as a whole—and *no one will notice*.

You *can* nurture a deeper understanding of just why PLC teams are so critical to the school culture and help those teams find their internal team balance for movement into the flow channel. The benefit of working as a professional learning community is not just increased task accomplishment. It is about coming together in a community for an optimal work experience that surpasses your expectations, places others in the flow channel, and creates great results for student performance. As a leader it is your responsibility to mobilize, focus, inspire, and regularly take actions that renew the energy of those you lead. It is about becoming and being a *professional*. It is about leading and teaching others how to fully engage in the promise and hope of their chosen profession.

# Study Guide ▪ ▪ ▪ ▪ ▪

Visit **go.solution-tree.com/plcbooks** to download this study guide and the worksheets mentioned in it.

## *Examining My Leadership Perspective*

1. How would you describe what happens on your best and worst leadership days? Download the worksheet *My Best and Worst Leadership Days*. What title would you choose for each day—ideal/actual? Dream/nightmare? Calm/disturbed? Utopian/dystopian? What does the comparison reveal about the nature of your current leadership life?

2. Do you ever feel the Red Queen is visiting you? *You have to run as fast as you can just to stay in the same place.* How do you respond when this happens? Take the *Hurry Sickness Checklist* test. How many yes answers do you have? How do you plan to address those symptoms?

3. How do you distribute your time and energy across Quadrant I and Quadrant II behaviors? How do you recognize that you are drifting into Quadrant III behaviors? What strategies do you use to stop the drift? What do you do when you notice those in your leadership area drifting into Quadrant III behaviors?

4. Do you pride yourself on the use of technology? On being a multi-tasker? Examine how your self-perception in these two areas affects the way in which you work and the way in which you interact with those you lead.

5. What factors motivate you in your leadership life? How do you communicate the value of these factors to those you lead?

6. *Because I can* syndrome affects many leaders. Are you or others in your leadership area affected? What kind of conversation do you think would develop if you were to include *because I can* as a topic at a team meeting?

7. Do you consider yourself to be an effective model of reflective and balanced leadership? Why or why not? How do you work to strengthen your leadership capabilities? To what extent do you share these efforts with those you lead? How do you plan to use material in this chapter to make changes in your leadership life?

## *Extending My Leadership Perspective*

1. Have your team complete the *Task Priority Management Tool* worksheet. Together with members of your team, compare the priority tasks,

the rationale for each, and plans for accomplishing them. What does this activity reveal about the team's focus on service to what is really important? How will you use this information to guide planning for the future?

2.  To what extent do you think that PLC team members are not fully engaged in their work life every day? What are the consequences for individuals who fail to meet their responsibilities? How can you address this matter with them? With the team?

3.  How would you rate the nature of communications within your leadership team? What are the strengths or limitations? To what extent does trust affect the quality of communications? What impact does the use of email have on team communications? How will you use these observations to foster a collegial environment within the team? You may want the team to discuss the handout *Dos and Don'ts for Email Use*.

4.  Use the figure *Professional Learning Community Flow* (page 138) as a diagnostic tool with your leadership team to help members determine where the team currently fits on the flow channel. Place sticky dots on the chart for each learning team. What themes emerge from the discussion? What plan do you have to address controversies that may arise from the discussion? Based on the outcome of the discussion, you might find it useful to examine your own behavior in relation to the five strategies that facilitate movement toward and along the flow channel. See the worksheet *Five Strategies for Movement Toward and Along the Flow Channel*.

5.  Invite your leadership team to answer this question: How would you describe the physical and emotional energy of our professional learning community? To what extent are team members' energy descriptions consistent? Present the graphic *The PLC Energy Quadrants* (page 143). How does the concept of the energy quadrants relate to service and sharing culture improvement in your PLC?

CHAPTER 5

*The Discipline of*

# Inspiration
# and Influence

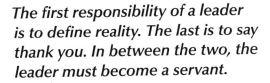

*The first responsibility of a leader is to define reality. The last is to say thank you. In between the two, the leader must become a servant.*

—Max De Pree

In the end, all I really wanted to say—all I really could say—was thank you. It would be my fifteenth and final message as superintendent to the faculty and staff at Stevenson High School District 125. After twenty-one years at Stevenson and thirty-five years of teaching and leading, I was leaving a district I had grown to love, to begin a new era of teaching, leading, and learning with others. I had written and rewritten this final message five times. And it felt so final. So surreal. Twenty-one times in a row, I had come back each August to start a new school year at Stevenson. But I would not be back for a twenty-second time. This was it—my final moment to share my thoughts, feelings, words, and actions with a faculty and staff that I loved very much. The auditorium was filled with a lot of school heroes whom I respected and admired.

It was June 6, 2007. The faculty and staff also had a lot on their minds as they entered the auditorium. End-of-year grades and reports were due the next day. The summer school transition teams needed to be ready for next week. One-third of the district campus was shutting down for construction work, and many faculty work areas and classrooms were being furiously boxed up—"bagged, tagged, and dragged" to cars and homes. The dust was flying; activities and decisions were being made at a staccato pace. It was a circus-like atmosphere, as everyone had to stop at 1:45 p.m. and come together for our end-of-year celebration (part of our Stage 6 cycle for continuous improvement). As is typical for the end of the school year, there was no real "normal" as we gathered together one last time.

We recognized our five-, ten-, fifteen-, twenty-, twenty-five-, and thirty-year employees. We recognized the Super Pats who individually or as a team went above and beyond in order to benefit students and fellow colleagues over the past semester. And then it was time to say farewell to the dedicated faculty and staff leaving the district. They would not be opening their boxes next August to start a new year at Stevenson. Some of them had given twenty-five to thirty years of their professional life to the district. Soon they would be opening their boxes at home. Their journey, their legacy, and their direct impact on the culture of our school was over. I had gone through this saying-goodbye ritual every June for many years. Only this time, it was more personal—I was one of those leaving. I kept thinking, *What are we leaving behind?* What have we given those who are staying to remember us by?

There is a sudden sadness in knowing you are no longer part of the future plans. Soon my leadership would be reduced to a fading memory. What could I possibly say that would matter to anyone on this busy last day of school? After four to five attempts to write the message, I was reduced to saying thank you. It had occurred to me that if I was looking to write and design a final message to remember me by, it was a little late. I had had twenty years—more than 4,500 days' worth of opportunities to build any type of inspiration and influence legacy. To paraphrase Robert Quinn (2004), it seemed to me that you "build the bridge as you walk on it." I had left a legacy and built my bridge, one way or the other—and so have you. You build your legacy bridge each day as you choose how to lead in your personal sphere of influence.

On the stage, I was aware that it was also an emotional day for others who were leaving the district that year, as well as those who would be leaving in the next two to three years. This day was on their horizon too. They only had a few years left to build an answer to the question, what will I give you to remember me by?

Also in attendance that day were faculty and staff members who weren't even born when I started teaching. For them, this day was too far down the road to touch. Legacy building, inspirational teaching, and leading and lifting student improvement were just starting for them. They had plenty of time to figure it out. *How would I reach them?* I wondered. Why bother them with a legacy-building speech? Why worry them about a distant dilemma? Because I knew from experience that the end of service could happen to them at any time. We don't always get to name the terms of our own *what will I give you to remember me by* moment.

That day, I spoke about the importance of every adult, every faculty and staff member, to take seriously his or her daily, monthly, and yearly pursuit of legacy building—of learning and leading together. For the fifteen of us retiring, it was too late. We had chosen our path, built our bridges of inspiration and influence—*or not.* In the end, that legacy was all we had to leave behind. How well did we serve others, and how well did we serve our school organization? I knew that legacies usually vary widely among retiring faculty and staff. Not everyone serves as a great model of inspiration and influence. For some, inspiration and influence just weren't the path they chose, or perhaps a path they didn't know how to choose.

Yet for those staff remaining in service—for those who would continue to breathe life into the school district and its various programs for student learning and growth over the next decade and more—it wasn't too late. They could choose to live legacy-building PLC lives—lives of no regret—or not. They still had time. And that day, in my own way, I tried to outline for them a vision of that path—a path of inspiration and influence.

As I spoke that day, the definition of the leadership discipline of inspiration and influence was in the back of my mind:

> **The leadership work of consciously creating an enduring organizational legacy through the daily building of effective PLC practices and behaviors**

# The PLC Leader's Legacy

It takes personal discipline as a teacher and leader to build an organizational legacy with others. *It doesn't happen by chance.* You will not lead and just happen to luck into a great legacy. Your area of influence—your N-S-E-W sphere of influence—the district, school, or school program of your area of leadership—will become legacy-worthy because, at some point, you intentionally realized that your work as a PLC school leader is much more than a job. You began to realize that your daily work, energy, actions, and reactions leave an imprint on the school organization and its people. Positive or negative, you are building a PLC legacy of influence and inspiration brick by brick every day. And before you know it, you are six, eleven, eighteen, or twenty-five years into establishing the foundation of your legacy. You look back and ask, How am I doing so far? And what criteria should I use, as a PLC leader, as the basis for knowing?

In this book, I have encouraged you to train more deeply, to spend time practicing specific leadership disciplines that will make the daily bricklaying worthwhile and not leave your PLC leadership legacy to chance. The four PLC leadership disciplines we have studied thus far provide insight into the criteria you should use to know whether your daily efforts in PLC leadership have had a positive impact. Each of these disciplines subsequently becomes part of your daily work that ultimately leads to an enduring legacy.

1. **Vision and values:** *The promise to yourself and others to develop and deliver a compelling picture of the school's future that produces energy, passion, and action in yourself and others*

   A primary legacy benefit to your work and training in the leadership discipline of shared vision development is clarity and coherence. Teachers, staff, parents, and students need you to be crystal clear each day. The vision brings coherence to your actions and your work. They need your communication to be clear around a simple but important message: Here is our shared vision for instruction, assessment, student growth, and development. Here is what I ask of you. Nothing less than your best effort and growth toward this vision is acceptable. This is a great summative phrase for your *what will I give you to remember me by* legacy as a PLC leader.

2. **Accountability and celebration:** *The promise to yourself and others to deliver specific improvement in student achievement results and to monitor stakeholder actions that will lead to those improved results, with consequences*

   A primary legacy benefit to your training in the leadership discipline of accountability and celebration is the development of many talented people who resolve the pockets of mediocre student performance throughout your area of school leadership. They turn the vision of improved student achievement into realized action and close the implementation gap toward research-affirmed best practices. The quest for meaningful adult and student growth begins inside this discipline: everyone matters—every student, parent, and colleague matters—and we must work to seek out and erase inequities in our student and adult learning experiences. This is another great summative phrase for your *what will I give you to remember me by* legacy as a PLC leader.

3. **Service and sharing:** *The promise to yourself and to others to demonstrate personal accountability to the shared vision and to all who may be affected by your thoughts, words, actions, and inactions*

   A primary legacy benefit to your training in the leadership discipline of service and sharing is the successful relationships that foster improved student achievement and character. A culture of collaborative social justice emerges that seeks to erase hidden as well as more obvious inequities in student learning experiences—and the PLC culture becomes sustainable, with or without you.

   As you lead by serving, you enable a culture of trust that eliminates the "us versus them" mindset. You build trust by listening, by respecting and integrating the thoughts of others into your own belief system. Trust building becomes a daily and dynamic process you never take for granted. It is an exhausting but worthwhile endeavor to strive to say, I did not always agree with you, but I knew I could trust your intentions and your integrity for my growth and development. Here is another great summative phrase for your *what will I give you to remember me by* legacy as a PLC leader.

4. **Reflection and balance:** *The promise to yourself and to others to intentionally and strategically engage in and disengage from high-energy activities*

   A primary legacy benefit to your training in the leadership discipline of reflection and balance is the understanding that life is reflective movement. Optimal experiences keep you moving forward and seeking continuous improvement in the flow channel. Another benefit is the opportunity to cultivate a few very close friends who will help you live a balanced life between Quadrants I and II. Those in your N-S-E-W spheres need you to live a leadership life that is fully engaged and that models the internal balance of positive energy leadership: You aimed high. You expected much from us. You sometimes failed to meet the ideals of a PLC as a leader, but you never stopped trying.

You gave us permission to fail, learn, and grow. This is another great summative phrase for your *what will I give you to remember me by* legacy as a PLC leader.

On the stage that June afternoon, I closed by saying, "Don't be afraid of failure and change as you focus your work energy to turn vision into action. Choose with no regret—come to work engaged and energized every day. Live and work to complete your PLC legacy bridge one brick, one day at a time—by serving others in our school district for the purpose of adult and student learning. Our school organization has become a place where great journeys begin. For me, it became a place where great journeys also end." With that statement, twenty-one years of school site leadership at Stevenson ended.

Your brick-by-brick, one-day-at-a-time PLC leadership legacy also requires you to embrace the conscious choice to connect with those in your N-S-E-W spheres in a way that leads to an enduring *organizational* influence long after you no longer serve and lead. That is the intent of the discipline of inspiration and influence: *the leadership work of consciously creating an enduring organizational legacy through the daily building of PLC practices and behaviors.*

In the discipline of influence and inspiration, our vision and action plans collide with our legacy: the facts of our past behavior that remain in the minds of others and are embedded in the values of the organization. What you *plan to do* for the future should align with what *you leave behind* as a leader. This alignment is the secret to legacy building. You cannot reach your full potential as a leader, or help others reach theirs, until you become intentional about imagining how the organization would look in three, five, or ten years, based on your actions *today*. Failure to make this connection is often the cause of organizational mediocrity. It is why so many schools and school programs fail to significantly improve. Yes, legacy building is about who you want to become as a leader. But more importantly, it is about what you want the *school organization* to become. What will be the *school organization legacy* you leave behind? Will it be positive or negative? Will it endure or fade away? Long after the Level 5 leaders like you have left the building, will there be a positive residue from the impact of your leadership work?

To develop an enduring legacy, you need *all* adults within the school organization, especially the faculty and administration, to train for and pursue the PLC leadership discipline of inspiration and influence. So, how do you improve in the discipline of inspiration and influence? How do you train to take legacy-building actions now that will result in great moments of reflection when your leadership journey comes to an end? Just as you live for the experience of a Quadrant I, in-the-flow work life, you leave hoping for a leadership legacy that endures within the school organization and its inheritors, long after all are gone. There are three legacy practices that PLC leaders commit to: they respond to failure, they prevent deep regret, and they choose the path of enduring leadership inspiration.

# Legacy Practice 1: Responding to Failure

I have the opportunity and privilege to work with a wide variety of schools across the country. I am often asked to provide feedback on the culture of the school, the implementation level of professional learning communities, or the level and quality of innovation and creativity by the adults in the school. As Pfeffer and Sutton (2006) point out, the best diagnostic question a leader can ask is, What happens when people fail? What happens when teachers or teacher teams try an innovative idea that fails? What happens when students or parents fail to meet the expectations of learning?

> We concluded that when we wanted to learn a lot about a company quickly—wanted a fast hint about whether an organization's leader had the attitude of wisdom, whether a company used practices that were supported by the best evidence, and whether conditions were ripe for turning all that knowledge into action, we both asked the same diagnostic questions: what happens when people fail? (p. 232)

A hallmark of professional learning community leadership is your intentional and positive response to failure at all levels of the school organization. The systemic, swift, and intentional adult response to any level of student failure is one of the four critical questions every PLC learning team must answer. According to the All Things PLC website (2011), adult leadership teams ask, "How will we provide students with additional time and support in a timely, directive, and systemic way when they experience difficulty in their learning?" Your ongoing leadership response to this question reveals the truth about how the school responds to the world of student misunderstandings, errors, and apathy to learning. Student failure that is not used as part of a reflective learning experience hurts everyone. Your level of leadership tolerance for student failure reveals your wisdom in using student mistakes as a tool to improve the ongoing formative cycle of learning in your area of school leadership. Does the culture embrace student errors, require students to become reflective practitioners, and require student participation in a formative assessment learning process? Intentional, required student participation in response to failure is a legacy-building practice of extraordinary PLC leaders.

In every school, there is also a parallel leadership response for adult misunderstandings, errors, and risk taking. Does your leadership inspire or discourage adult risk taking? Can adults within your N-S-E-W sphere of influence take risks, make mistakes, and learn and grow from those experiences without punitive judgment? The level of innovation and renewal success in your district, school, or program area of school leadership depends on the degree of focused risk a team is willing to take and the confidence of the team in a positive leadership response when failure occurs.

Carol Dweck (2006), author of *Mindset: The New Psychology of Success*, summarizes her decades of research around two distinct mindsets of response to failure. These distinctions help the PLC leader to better understand why some adults have a difficult time responding to failure. Adults with a *growth* mindset believe their "talents, aptitudes, interests and temperament can change and grow over time" (p. 7). Growth-mindset adults embrace learning team challenges and failure as an opportunity to improve. In contrast, adults with a *fixed mindset* believe the qualities of talent, aptitude, interests, and temperament are "carved in stone" (p. 6). These adults see every failure as an indictment of their worthiness. For fixed-mindset adults who believe these important qualities cannot be developed or grown, failure indicates permanently limited abilities or unworthiness as a faculty member or an administrator in the school.

Dweck indicates that "the passion for stretching yourself and sticking to it, even (or especially) when it is not going well, is a hallmark of the growth mindset" (p. 7). The growth mindset is a major premise of the PLC culture for adults and students alike as they move along in the flow channel described in chapter 4 (page 137) and thus should be the focal point of the risk-taking measures a PLC leader should pursue. PLC leaders help those who are stuck in a fixed-mindset response move to a growth-mindset response to failure.

To help fixed-mindset adults become comfortable with learning from failure, inspirational and influential leaders promote and nurture a culture of risk taking. How well do you promote risk taking? The following four risk-taking strategies will provide a litmus test of your current legacy building and can be used to promote a growth-mindset culture.

## *Embrace Risk-Taking Language*

How is the idea of risk spoken about in your school? Take the time to notice the phrases about risk that individuals use. Examples might be "minimizing the risk," "running the risk," "reducing the risk," "risk-prone," "risk-averse," "balancing the risks," "spreading the risk," "worth the risk," "focused risk," "fear of risk," "risk excitement," and "risky actions." The central tenet of the PLC leadership response to failure, either student or adult, is a paradox: *To risk nothing is to risk everything.* To not try new things, to not create opportunities to fail, is to stop becoming a true learning organization.

Does your risk-taking vocabulary declare, "Let's learn from our failures, let's learn from our mistakes, let's learn from our effort, and let's grow together"? The PLC growth mantra should be "We may not know how to do this new task right now, but together, with time and effort, our PLC team members will learn how to do it and do it well." Your leadership messages must promote a culture for focused and safe risk taking by the faculty and staff. Is growth and improvement language a cultural norm in your area of school leadership? PLC leaders monitor for and promote positive risk-taking language.

## *Embrace Risk-Taking Champions*

Who are your risk-taking leaders in the school? Who are the adults fully engaged in a growth mindset, willing to take risks and reach their full potential? Who are the adults who fully understand how to experiment within boundaries and through experience, trial and error, and reflection on results—those individuals willing to take risks to close student learning gaps and improve student learning?

An early leadership lesson for me on the issue of embracing risk-taking champions occurred during the redesigning of a mathematics course that had consistently high student failure rates. Rather than create risk-taking engagement and intervention strategies for the course, we continued to verify—year in and year out—that students just could not "do the math" in this course. We had a fixed mindset.

And then I found Neal Roys—a risk-taking champion and growth-mindset teacher. Neal was brilliant, with the heart and compassion for students and a passion for technology. Together we created a new name for the course—*Transition to College Mathematics* (at least the course name sounded like it had a purpose). I gave Neal four guidelines or boundaries for his creative risk-taking changes in the course:

1. The course standards/outcomes could not eliminate content standard expectations for these potentially college-bound students.

2. Preparation for the ACT and SAT was required.

3. The course pedagogy needed to be motivating and engaging for all students.

4. The course needed to integrate technology as a tool for learning in daily lesson design.

It is important to stop here for a moment and examine the relationship of trust between Neal (the teacher) and me (the leader). Notice my statement: *I gave Neal four guidelines or boundaries.* Creativity and risk taking, and innovation and new ideas, are best when constrained. If not constrained, these efforts are bound to have random results for failure or success. Neal welcomed the constraints on his creativity, worked with another teacher and me to design a new course to meet those guidelines, and enjoyed the freedom to create—knowing that as long as he met the criteria, he would have my full support—whether the result was success or failure.

This inventive teacher created a problem-solving, technology-oriented (every student was given a graphing calculator) course with meaningful and connected applications that diminished the dropout problem. As a result of his gift of teaching complex ideas using simple explanations and connections, students flocked to the course. He also led the knowledge and skill development of the special education and ESL teachers on how to use the technology. The end results were a lowering of the failure and dropout rate from 53 percent to 18 percent in two years, an increase in student enrollment in this capstone alternative course, and better preparation for college. Neal was a game changer. His work laid the foundation of high-quality senior alternatives for the district; later, other champion risk-takers took over and moved the course to an even more sophisticated project-based learning alternative. Embrace your game changers—give them reasonable boundaries, and let them fly!

## *Embrace Deep Relational Risk Taking*

Professional learning communities require personal risk and willingness to be vulnerable with others. As we take risks as part of a team, we move closer to our full potential. We experience true joy and pain with the people we work with, care about, and learn to respect. We share in the triumphs of our team and its members—and the tragedies, too. We learn to listen for signs of a fixed mindset that might limit the potential growth and risk-taking tenacity of the team.

When my first real school leader and immediate boss, Lee Yunker, died of brain cancer at age 53 (I was 43 at the time), I was crushed at the pain of his loss. Lee had taught me how to take research-affirmed risks in the classroom without fear of reprisal. He led by his own example, and for six years, side by side, we taught, laughed, and learned from our mistakes together. Lee taught me that humility invites risk and egotism destroys it. I suppose that was why I knew back on opening day in 1986 (my leadership debut with the mathematics and science division of the school) that I would have no tolerance for egotistical people in my sphere of influence. We were going to become a risk-taking program—*humility required.* Growth mindset required. No limitations to possibility of improvement required.

Vulnerability arises when you commit to a culture of learning together. Becoming interdependent in a team brings risk: the risk of feeling let down and disappointed when others don't meet the expectations, the risk of letting others down if you don't meet their expectations. Risking the pain of being hurt *is* part of the journey. Lee's inspiration in my life was worth the risk. In turn, the success of taking that risk helped me to become a leader who would reach out, care for, and take risks with hundreds of other educators during my leadership life. Lee did not get to choose his retirement day—but his legacy was one of research-affirmed risk taking and a growth mindset. He gave me a terrific legacy to remember him by, and his influence on me and many others endures to this day, almost twenty years later.

## *Embrace Risk Taking With Planned Abandonment*

As PLC leaders respond to failure, they are willing to abandon the old that is not working well, hold onto the old that is working well, and make way for new actions and new risks. Think of these actions as *planned abandonment.* An inherent paradox exists in your risk-taking response to failure. You must take risks that both add to and abandon current practices. You take risks on new actions you add to the current "stuff" you are doing. You expand capacity urgently. For example, typical professional development in your school (the new risk-taking effort) might feel like this:

> *We will implement and train on the new problem-solving elementary school math program. We will also receive professional development training to help support our Tier 1 and Tier 2 RTI efforts in grades K–5. And everyone will implement last year's literacy training for academic vocabulary as we continue our work with formative assessment building.*

To assume this much risk taking requires an accompanying leadership plan for systematic abandonment of other work-related tasks. Are there any concurrent practices that no longer provide evidence of viability for success? Can you move efficiently to let them go? Ultimately, all adults in a professional learning community understand that failure should be embraced as part of the *learning cycle.* One of the greatest and most consistent mistakes that newly formed PLC cultures make is attempting to do too much all at once. Part of maintaining a healthy risk-taking culture is following a systematic plan to abandon ineffective practices as you and your leadership team take on new risk-oriented activities.

What makes *team* learning and risk taking more vulnerable than *solitary* learning and risk taking is that the former is so *public.* Pfeffer and Sutton (2006) say it like this:

> We wish it were possible to live in a world where mistakes, setbacks, and errors never happen. We despise our own failures, it wounds us when people we care about suffer setbacks, and we even find ourselves feeling bad for people we dislike when they make mistakes. Failure hurts, it is embarrassing, and we would rather live without it. Yet there is no learning without failure. As we've seen, there is always a learning curve when an organization tries something new or trains people—including doctors and managers—to do something new. If you look at how the most effective systems in the world are managed, a hallmark is that when something goes wrong, people face the hard facts, learn what happened and why, and keep using those facts to make the system better. (p. 232)

Professional learning communities are all about *using the hard facts to make the school organization better.* Your legacy is revealed through the school's response to failure and its risk taking to close the gap on student and adult success. The discipline of inspiration and influence requires your intentional and positive embrace of learning from failure and mistakes in order to create a better "next year." Such actions improve your chances of living with no regrets, especially the regret of leadership inaction, such as the regret I felt after waiting seven years to actually enforce student-engaged learning in every classroom. Admit to and abandon failed practices, and begin to take risks on new research-affirmed actions today.

# Legacy Practice 2: Preventing Deep Regret

Have you or colleagues ever sent an email that, in the blink of the moment after you sent it, you immediately regretted? Maybe it was sent to the wrong person;

maybe it was sent in a moment of exhaustion, frustration, anger, or distraction. While I was superintendent, I once received a group email intended for another Tim in our school district. This other Tim happened to be the faculty union president at the time. The sender of the email had deep regret as it damaged the trust level of our relationship for a long time.

If you use Google Mail (Gmail), you have access to an email "regret preventer" called "Mail Goggles." Designed by Gmail engineer Jon Perlow, Mail Goggles requires you to verify and answer some simple math problems before you are allowed to send the email. Used primarily as a late-night and weekend feature, it slows down the possibility of sending an email you might otherwise regret, especially those late-night memos that you accidently send as a "reply all." Our school life doesn't have "leadership regret" goggles. The truth is we only have the moment we live in now, and time will not slow down or wait for us to do a few math computation problems before we hit "send." All of our actions and inactions are filled with potential for regret, and we can never redo yesterday. Time does not allow us to go backward, only forward. Do you have any regrets? I do. We all do. You cannot lead in the world of PLC leadership and not have a few regrets. You are human, after all.

Leadership growth in the discipline of inspiration and influence begins with your response to failure and mistakes, your willingness to pursue risks, and your understanding that unless you learn from your mistakes and failures, you will look in the rearview mirror of your leadership life and experience deep regret. But you can avoid situations that lead to regret: you can become a growth-mindset leader and learn from your mistakes. Ask yourself, what do I need to do now to prevent deep regret later? As you grow in the discipline of inspiration and influence, you intentionally become more adept at living fully engaged in the present leadership moment, which establishes barriers to regrettable actions. You have your own built-in "regret goggles" that help you to see how your actions or inactions *now* could cause you deep regret later. And in our profession, *now* happens again and again and again every year. You must get intentional to prevent regret from the lessons learned each year.

Each school year is unique, but each school year also provides a renewed opportunity to do better in the next cycle of your work and leadership experience. When all the years roll by and you are standing at the end of your career, you might ask yourself two questions: Did I pay attention to others deeply? Did I build trust into my area of school leadership?

## *Pay Attention to Others Deeply*

As a leader and as a teacher, you cannot inspire others unless you are crystal clear about the exceptionality of your purpose in life. Knowing that school leadership is part of your passion is essential to persevering and pushing through moments of doubt and resistance. Is it possible there are individuals you could have loved more deeply, encouraged more often, or been more attuned to? This element of regret is tightly related to the discipline of reflection and balance as an ongoing part of your daily life. "Someday I'll get around to noticing and paying attention to others better," you say. But someday never comes, and then even the chance for someday is gone.

I had a "someday" leadership moment about ten years into my leadership role as the director of mathematics and science. The moment occurred on a Friday at 2:00 p.m. as I was about to enter into a postconference with a teacher who had about ten years left in what had been a promising teaching career, but had recently faded into hopelessness and burnout. After three days of observation of his sixth-hour classroom, we were about to meet for his postobservation conference. It had occurred to me that I needed to figure out how to approach the situation so that in the aftermath of our discussion, neither one of us would have any regrets.

To some extent, he had lost his love for teaching. He was failing to love his students deeply. As a leader to his north, I had a right to be angry over his verbal treatment of students, his display of apathy toward preparation, and his somewhat cynical view of administration. His career and his vocation were at a fork in the road—either his life was about the right thing (teaching children well), or he had made a big mistake and his work life had been dedicated to something he couldn't or wouldn't love and care about. The issue was urgent because he was suffering, and in turn, so were his students. My response to his failure, my response to his future, needed to be a "no regrets" response. So I decided to take the high road and pay attention to him more deeply. That decision was my "someday" moment.

I ignored my three days of observation notes and asked him to recall a time when he loved teaching. He talked about it for quite a while. I then asked him to describe the moment he became aware that his love for students and for teaching his subject area had started to erode. We agreed to use the weekend to create a plan of hope for a no-regrets future. He would list five actions he could take moving forward, and so would I. On Monday, we would compare our lists and work together to rekindle his love of teaching. We collaborated on a plan for how he could live forward with a no-regrets professional life: how he might be able to change the community's perception of him and, over time, win back the hearts of his students. This is where the cyclical nature of the school year really helps. As the following school year unfolded, his new set of students had no direct institutional memory. They had heard he was a mean-spirited, grumpy teacher, but they were still new to him as he was to them.

To his credit, this teacher spent the next four years of his professional life choosing to make no-regrets decisions—laughing more, learning more, listening to his colleagues, appreciating his students and his family. He joined a PLC teaching team that was at a more accelerated level than the one he had been on, and he thrived with the new content challenge and his new colleagues who were supportive and encouraging. He had chosen to finish well. And then one September evening, he did not wake up from his sleep. His chance to choose a no-regrets life was over. His retirement day was not to come. At his funeral, *hundreds* of students and parents were in attendance. All of them praised his teaching, kindness, and love for students. He left behind a more recent legacy of loving others deeply. He made the decision to finish well—before it was too late—with no regrets. How awesome. How fearless. How courageous.

What is your *someday I'll get around to noticing and paying attention to others better* leadership moment?

### Be a Trust Builder

I suspect that like me, you have been on both sides of the trust equation. I have been in school leadership situations where trust was violated and abandoned, and I experienced the negative effects of those relationships. More often than not though, I have experienced the remarkable PLC benefits of trusting others and allowing them the opportunity to own their work and results. I have also had the benefit of being trusted. It gave me confidence in my work as a school leader. Yet building trust within your area of school leadership is an elusive and unending pursuit. And once built, trust must never be taken for granted. Can you build your trust leading skills? Yes. You can inspire trust. You can cultivate it and restore it. Trust rekindles the inner spirit of your leadership work and limits the opportunities for regret. It is essential to building successful PLC teams.

*Trust begins with a personal commitment to respect others.* Everyone matters—every student, parent, and colleague. Respect develops when you, as a PLC leader, understand the strengths and weaknesses of each person in your sphere of influence, and you integrate them into the work of the learning team and the school program. Trust means you are willing to really listen to others as you monitor their actions and behaviors. Trust does not mean indifference to the work of others. It means respecting the work, listening first, and really noticing what is going on.

*Trust is built on kept promises.* I learned this lesson the hard way early in my leadership career. In meetings, I would often use the phrase "I will try to get it done." Of course, those in my leadership sphere assumed correctly that I was making a promise to action: that I would get it done. However, in my mind, I was only saying, "I will *try* to get it done," and that let me off the hook to actually do something. One day one of my staff members came into my office and said, "You are losing credibility with the faculty because you keep telling us you are going to get things done, and they aren't done yet. Don't promise if you can't deliver." And then she walked out. She was right. From that moment forward, I was very careful to measure what I promised and to make sure I delivered what I promised. Few things chip away more at trust than broken promises.

Monitor your PLC learning teams on this issue. The vision of the school organization serves as the neutral authority that allows trust to flourish. As discussed in chapter 2, turning vision into action requires that members of the PLC address adult behaviors that are inconsistent with the vision of the school or program (see page 50). When you are able to divert difficult conversations away from the person and toward the actions that are inconsistent with the vision, you set the stage for trust to develop. It becomes clear that you are not out to "get" anyone but rather to protect the moral purpose of the work.

*For trust to be sustained, you must demonstrate competence—both relational and technical/pedagogical.* This requires you to become strong in the disciplines of leadership described in this book. Your personal integrity will lead the school to pursue the truth of things that you just flat-out know will work. Those in your N-S-E-W sphere can more often than not count on you to do the right thing, regardless of legalistic rules and regulations that sometimes constrain you. Sometimes the *right thing* is part of your instinct and the instinct of the wise leaders of your school or district, and sometimes it is a result of your hard work to develop your knowledge and relational capacity as a leader.

*Trust is built on a foundation of reciprocal accountability.* This is why establishing a clear and effective accountability and assessment cycle of continuous improvement has such value. This cycle builds mutual trust structures—with accountability that results and work effort will match. You can *trust* that adult actions will result in good things. And those good ideas can emerge from anyone or anywhere in the school organization.

Building trust, then, is one of your major no-regrets responsibilities. Although organizational and personal trust can be elusive, trust is earmarked by persistence, patience, discipline, and grace. *The best indicator of trust is how hard you lean on those in your N-S-E-W spheres and how hard they lean on you.* The greater the lean, the greater the trust. Stephen M. R. Covey (2006) provides this great tip for transparency in developing trust in your leadership behavior in *The Speed of Trust*:

> Tell the truth in a way people can verify. Get real and genuine. Be open and authentic. Err on the side of disclosure. Operate on the premise of "What you see is what you get." Don't have hidden agendas. Don't hide information. (p. 322)

Being transparent is a required PLC leadership behavior for building trust and motivation within the team. Always remember that this ongoing pursuit of trust is based first and foremost on your honesty and integrity as a leader.

# Legacy Practice 3: Choosing the Path of Enduring Inspiration

Your legacy of inspiration and influence establishes a direction, and that direction is built on a foundation of truth. Your leadership pursuit of the truth and of research and actions that correlate to improving student achievement is essential. Truth for "what works" has to be your first level of quality and can only become part of your legacy if you model it for others. Failure to lead on this point produces incoherence, unfocused action, and poor results in the school as a whole.

Ask most seasoned school leaders—especially those in the arena of PLC school leadership—what their greatest fear as a leader is, and the most frequently given response will perhaps surprise you. Their biggest fear is *endurance.* How do you endure and sustain a high level of inspiration year in and year out? Think about those individuals in your sphere of influence. Inspirational leaders lift your spirit. You have a right to an inspirational leadership presence in your life and a responsibility to become one for others. How do you maintain a leadership spirit of enduring inspiration for all those in your N-S-E-W sphere? Several practices will help you maintain your effort in this leadership discipline over time: surrounding yourself with inspiring people, being part of an inspiring team, forgiving gracefully, participating in inspiring events, and paying attention to physical disciplines.

## *Hang Out With Exceptionally Inspiring People*

A first step to ensuring you stay in an inspired and motivated state is to hang out with exceptionally inspiring people. Who are these people in your leadership world? Who directly or indirectly inspires you to commit to full engagement in your work—year in and year out? You need to identify these people and then tell them. They need to know that part of their leadership role is to inspire your work, hold you accountable to your work, and become one of your loving critics. These exceptional people may be in your N-S-E-W sphere. They may be in your professional or personal life. And in some aspect relevant to you, they are probably "ahead of you" in both relational knowledge and competence knowledge. They are leaders who will pull you forward.

One exceptionally inspiring leader for me was a physics teacher named Jim McGrath. I was 35 when I met him, and he was 51. He had a quality of wisdom that served me well over the years. Although he was technically in my south sphere (I was his supervisor), he had been a school leader years ago—he had been in my shoes. And more importantly, I learned early on I could trust him. I had confidence that he had my best interests in mind. When you trust someone, communication flows quickly, and there is a comfortable exchange of information. Trust is the social glue that holds relationships together. I knew with Jim that I could trust his motives, his wisdom, and his insights—his encouragement and his cautionary advice guided me. Jim enjoyed being my mentor and participating in our early morning banter about issues that were often a puzzle to me in my leadership life.

In my north sphere was a wonderful woman named Shirley Frye. She had the gift of noticing others and lifting their spirits with her words, notes, cards, and attention to detail. She was a national icon in mathematics—a president of the National Council of Teachers of Mathematics and a leader of the national standards movement during the 1990s. She taught me how to appreciate and notice others by being a servant first. I hung out with Shirley whenever I could, just hoping to learn more from her leadership model. She was a model of patience and grace, and as a young leader I was trying get better at both of those practices.

And in my east-west sphere was Jerry Cummins, a colleague, coauthor, and friend. Jerry was one of those relational school leaders who provided inspiration to everyone in his presence. It was his gift. We first met in 1980, and I quickly decided to intentionally merge our professional and personal lives. We became fast friends, and over the years we shared many triumphs and tragedies. He became one of my loving critics, helping me to stay humble and focused in my leadership growth and teaching me how to be more thoughtful and engaging with others. Jerry's inspiration led to my own personal commitment to *enjoy* the leadership journey more and to not be quite so demanding of others. If I was able to lead from an inspired state, much of the credit goes to the foundation of accountability and support I received from Jerry's inspiration, humor, and friendship.

Who is your Jim McGrath, Shirley Frye, or Jerry Cummins? Do such individuals know it is their job to inspire you? Be sure to tell them. Stay connected to them. You cannot ignore those who lift your spirits.

## Be Part of a Team of Inspiring People

No longer is it sufficient for a teacher or school leader at any level to possess content knowledge and relational knowledge about *students* only. Leaders must also become masters of *relational knowledge for interaction* with other *adults*. A second step to ensuring you stay in an inspired or motivated state is to make sure you are part of a team of inspiring people. If you want to stay motivated over the long haul, surround yourself with people who give you a positive emotional jolt every time they walk into the room—people with *social* intelligence. Goleman (2007) describes social intelligence as much more than being *about* our relationships; it is also about being *in* them. He states:

> The social responsiveness of the brain demands that we be wise, that we realize how not just our moods but our very biology is being driven by the other people in our lives—and in turn, it demands that we take stock of how we affect other people's emotions and biology. Indeed, we can take the measure of a relationship in terms of a person's impact on us, and ours on them. (p. 11)

Early in our evolution into authentic professional learning communities at Stevenson, I had several faculty members who did not give me or their colleagues a positive emotional jolt whenever they walked into the room. In fact, they were polar opposites—gossips, close-minded, secretive, easily defensive, and unwilling to share. Their impact on the relational culture of our school program area was toxic at best. As the leader, I could not ignore how they were affecting the "biology" of our faculty and staff.

One such trust-buster was a perfectionist (in the negative sense) with little tolerance for the thoughts and insights of others. She had relationally sharp elbows, was easily defensive, didn't want to share, and didn't want to hear about her attitude. It was the rest of the team that had the problem, not her. Trust grows with a personal commitment to respect others, and she was failing to make that commitment. As the leader, I had to decide what to do. To build organizational trust meant having very low tolerance of trust-busting behaviors. So I confronted her. On a snowy winter day in my office, I held a figurative mirror up to her face and told her how her attitude, words, and actions were impacting her peers and me; how her behavior failed to respect and recognize the gifts, strengths, and talents of her team; and that she needed to listen to her colleagues and take their thoughts and advice seriously. She needed to trust others. And then I told her that I was no longer going to be her friend until she made these changes. She stole the joy from the journey, and I couldn't be part of that. If she could find a way to listen to others, to trust others, then maybe we could be friends again. She was not happy.

Yet at the heart of any level of organizational fidelity lies truth telling with grace. This teacher and I eventually became good friends, and her growth in relational competence led to her eventual leadership of one of our academic teams. Through hard work she learned that connecting with others required mutual empathy in which people are attuned to one another, in which colleagues "experience being experienced" (Goleman, 2007, p. 29). It is hard work to build mutual trust and requires a great deal of grace in the workplace, but it is a good way to be remembered when your legacy-building days are over.

## Forgive Gracefully

A third step in maintaining an inspired or motivated leadership life is to learn to forgive gracefully. The very nature of communication and interplay among professional learning community teams during the course of a school year almost guarantees that some feelings will be hurt, someone will be wounded, and grace will be needed. Grace in the workplace is inspiring, and leaders must first show and model grace. Kouzes and Posner (2006) state it like this:

> The people we work with and count on are also human, and despite their best intentions, they don't always do what they say they will do. We need to give them the same opportunities we afford ourselves to try and fail and try again. We need to give them the chance to be the best they can be, even to be better than they thought they could be. We need to support them in their growth and help them to recognize that the journey is not about perfection but about becoming fully human. . . . Let's all have the humility to remember where we started and the humanity to offer others the same opportunities. (pp. 160–161)

Is there anyone in your current N-S-E-W leadership sphere who is carrying around a grudge? Is that person focused on payback? Has bitterness set in? Grace wins out in the workplace when we set down the grudges we are carrying around. Grace wins when we use forgiveness to help others become better people.

Toward the end of my superintendent leadership, I received a call regarding a major dispute between two faculty members. A teacher from one of our academic areas of the school needed a favor from one of our athletic coaches, and he refused to help her out. The favor was minor and concerned an early release from a practice for a specific student. He refused. These two teachers had known each other a long time. They talked it out, and he still refused. So I got involved. I asked the coach why he wouldn't help the teacher out. In a state of anger, he blurted, "Three years ago, she refused to change my son's grade from a B to an A. It's payback time!" I sat thinking, Wow! Three years ago. Long time to carry around a grudge. Had he ever talked to her about it? No. Holding onto that grudge had served him better than forgiving her gracefully.

In spirit-lifting leadership, everyone matters. Everyone also has to learn to forgive and to reconcile quickly. A three-year grudge can cause a lot of damage to the school culture. Do you have a grudge you need to let go?

## Participate in Inspiring Events

A fourth step to ensure you stay in an inspiring and motivated state is to participate in events that are exceptionally inspiring. What are those events for you? One quick test is to spend a week monitoring all of the events and activities you participate in. Create a simple chart and track whether each activity adds energy to or drains energy from your day. For example, leadership team meetings might add energy. Meeting with an angry parent might drain energy. (Visit **go.solution-tree .com/plcbooks** to download a *Weekly Energy Monitoring* chart.)

At the end of the week, which column is longer? What types of activities seem to give you energy? How can you become more intentional about increasing those activities that add energy and restructuring other activities to minimize the energy drain?

For example, a favorite inspiring activity for me each week was to visit the classrooms of several faculty members. Whenever I was feeling an energy drain, I would visit one of those classrooms and observe. It never failed to inspire me. I was inspired by the incredible work of these dedicated teaching professionals. I always left their classrooms fired up to do my work at a higher level in order to better serve them. And not surprisingly, I would try to work with them as often as possible, so as to benefit from that energy.

What are those exceptionally inspiring events for you? Make sure they become part of your weekly routine.

## Pay Attention to Physical Disciplines

There are not too many school leadership books that ask school leaders to pay attention to their physical disciplines. In fact, I have found this to be a very sensitive subject for many leaders. Yet as we discussed in chapter 4 on reflection and balance, the pace of your leadership days can leave you emotionally and physically exhausted. And the more out of shape you are, the more tired you are, and the less energy you will have for the demands of your fast-paced job. William McArdle, Frank Katch, and Victor Katch (2007) in *Exercise Physiology* indicate that you experience a 20 percent gain in the energy needed for your work life if you exercise daily and fulfill your sleep requirements. A healthy and rested you is essential to your ability to lead a Quadrant I work life each day (see page 147).

Jim Loehr's (2007) *The Power of Story* provides great insight into how to make a systematic effort to improve this energy-producing area of your leadership life. He identifies faulty assumptions we often make as we seek balance:

- It's okay with my family when I come home from work exhausted and disengaged. They appreciate all that I do for the school.

- I'm still young, so I can get away with doing things that are bad for my health. Someday I'm going to have to significantly change or face the consequences. But I've still got time.

- I have no time or energy to exercise. My job is just too time-consuming.

Ultimately, you choose the level of physical exercise and sleep you need to be fully engaged in your life. You choose the amount of Quadrant II low-energy time. And more often than not, you will abuse this choice. Your reasoning is the same day in and day out: I will exercise tomorrow; I will get more sleep tomorrow; I just can't take the time right now for these energy-producing activities. These choices continue to drain you, and eventually you cannot lead or serve anyone well.

Disciplined inspirational leaders monitor their physical well-being and the energy impact it has on their lives. Don't let yourself drift into a dangerous place of Quadrant III and Quadrant IV physical and emotional energy.

# PLC Leadership Inspiration Matters

One of my favorite interview questions for any level of hiring within our school organization over the years was, "We are about to hire you for the following school year. What on earth would possess anyone, students or adults, to *follow you?*" I always asked this question early in the interview, and depending on the response, the interview shortly ended or moved on. This question almost always elicited a pause followed by "That is a very good question," as respondents searched for the proper words.

Often, leaders are so focused on leading that they fail to consider, what does my leadership look and feel like from the followers' perspective—or in your case as a PLC leader, from the perspective of those in your N-S-E-W sphere? Remember, followership is not about positional authority as much as it is about whether or not someone will allow you to influence his or her thinking and beliefs.

Gallup conducted a poll of ten thousand U.S. adults on this issue in 2005–2006. An expanded follow-up poll in 2008 verified similar results. The poll asked a two-part question:

1.  What leader has the most positive influence in your daily life?

2.  Now, please list three words that best describe what *this person contributes to your life.* (as cited in Rath & Conchie, 2008, pp. 80–81)

Rath and Conchie (2008) reported the survey results in their book *Strengths Based Leadership.* What would cause those in your N, S, E, or W spheres to choose to follow your leadership? The findings of the Gallup poll identified four basic needs:

1.  **Trust.** People seek honesty, integrity, and respect. Those in your sphere of influence will choose your leadership if your "truth is your bond— you die keeping your promises" (p. 83).

2.  **Compassion.** Respondents used words like *caring, friendship, happiness,* and *love.* Those in your sphere of influence choose to stay in organizations when their "immediate supervisor genuinely cares about them as a person" (p. 86).

3.  **Stability.** Respondents used words like *strength, support,* and *peace.* Those in your sphere of influence need to have a "sense of confidence about where their career is headed and how the organization is doing" (p. 88).

4. **Hope.** Respondents used words like *direction*, *faith*, and *guidance*; this point highlights the importance of service and engagement with others.

PLC leaders desire to inspire others by calling them to a cause far greater than themselves and by understanding their needs. Those needs include trust, compassion, stability, and hope grounded in a clear vision of the future. Your efforts to inspire, notice, and develop others become your PLC legacy. And it matters.

Rath and Conchie (2008) go on to cite other Gallup studies that highlight the impact leaders can have throughout an organization. The Gallup poll found these statistics from the employees surveyed: if the leader (influencer) primarily ignores you or primarily focuses on your weaknesses, there is only a 9 percent chance you will be engaged in your work. If the leader (influencer) primarily focuses on your strengths, there is a 73 percent chance you will be engaged. This is a valuable understanding for teachers with students, and for school leaders with faculty and staff. Leadership that centers on being inspirational and attentive and focuses on strengths matters in the development of a fully engaged PLC work culture.

# PLC Leaders Are Remembered for What They Do for Others

So there I was, that final day at Stevenson. There you will be someday, too—finishing your final message to the faculty and staff as their leader. You will have to ask, what have I given those who are staying to remember me by?

Those in your N-S-E-W sphere won't remember you so much for what you did for yourself. They will remember what *you do for them*. Trust, compassion, stability, and hope are great gifts to give and receive. If you give and receive those qualities, those within your sphere of influence will be the inheritors of your work, and you will have built your legacy as you lived it.

One of the more influential leaders in my early school leadership life was John W. Gardner, Secretary of Health, Education, and Welfare under President Lyndon Johnson. He received the Presidential Medal of Freedom in 1964. He oversaw significant expansions of the Elementary and Secondary Education Act of 1965 and wrote significant works on leadership, including *No Easy Victories* (Gardner, 1969), *On Leadership* (Gardner, 1990) and *Living, Leading, and the American Dream* (Gardner, Gardner, & Moyers, 2003). In the 1992 article "The Secret Ailment," he sums up the goal of the journey as a professional learning community school leader:

> We cannot dream of a utopia in which all arrangements are ideal and everyone is flawless. Life is tumultuous—an endless losing and regaining of balance, a continuous struggle, never an assured victory. Nothing is ever finally safe. Every important battle is fought and re-fought. We need to develop a resilient, indomitable morale that enables us to face those realities and still strive for every ounce of energy to prevail. . . . We have to believe in ourselves, but we mustn't suppose the path will be easy. It's tough. (p. 50)

*Every important battle in your PLC leadership life will need to be fought and re-fought.* What a great statement about the perseverance to master the five leadership disciplines described in this book. This tenacity is a very distinctive aspect of PLC leadership. There will always be some resistance to and misinterpretations of the work expectations and demands of the professional learning community. Embrace that resistance, and never give up hope. Use every ounce of energy to pay attention to students and to all the adults—everyone in your N-S-E-W sphere. And know that although, as Gardner says, everyone will not be flawless and there will be no assured victories, you can *choose* to lead a more disciplined leadership life that will benefit you and all those whom you influence.

This is the role of a PLC leader—to pursue a disciplined life that results in others choosing to follow and be followed, despite human flaws and obstacles. You choose and build the story of how you will be remembered every day, one brick at a time. Your leadership story will end someday, but your message will linger on. May we never forget it.

# Study Guide ▪ ▪ ▪ ▪ ▪

Visit **go.solution-tree.com/plcbooks** to download this study guide and the worksheets mentioned in it.

## *Examining My Leadership Perspective*

1. At this point in your leadership career, are you thinking about the legacy you will leave? Why or why not? How would you like to be remembered as a leader? In one sentence, describe the *what I will give you to remember me by* message of your PLC leadership life.

2. How would you rate your current level of leadership skill in each of the four disciplines described in the previous chapters—vision and values, accountability and celebration, service and sharing, and reflection and balance? In which discipline are your skills the strongest? The weakest? How do you plan to use your stronger skills to help you build the areas needing improvement? What time frame have you set to improve your leadership skills?

3. What is it about your leadership work that inspires you every day? How does that source of inspiration enhance your ability to embrace failure? To encourage risk taking? To build trust? To avoid being judgmental? To forgive graciously? To express appreciation?

4. What regrets have you experienced as a leader? Do you tend to dwell on the factors that contributed to those regrets? If so, how does that affect your performance as a leader? What insights about preventing regret have you gained from reading this chapter?

5. What advice would you give to someone just beginning a career as a school leader?

## *Extending My Leadership Perspective*

1. In your leadership role you are likely to encounter skeptics, cynics, opposers, and trust-busters—individuals whose actions impede progress in realizing the shared vision and contribute to disaffection in the team. Use the worksheet *Skeptics, Cynics, Opposers, and Trust-Busters* to identify all colleagues within your area of leadership who fit into each of these categories. Which of the leadership strategies you have read about in this book provide you with insights into how to work with these colleagues?

2. As a leader, you likely interview prospective candidates for positions within your leadership area. What would you like to find out from the candidates about their suitability for becoming part of your leadership team? What do you expect to be revealed if you ask, "We are about to hire you for the following school year. Why would anyone, students or adults, follow *you?*"

# The Professional Learning Community as a School Movement

*Live as if you were to die tomorrow. Learn as if you were to live forever.*

—Mahatma Gandhi

In 1986, I arrived on the school leadership scene relatively young and raring to go, with no idea of what it meant to be a *disciplined* professional learning community leader. I had just completed thirteen years of teaching in complete isolation from other adults, and rather enjoyed not depending too much on anyone else for doing what I thought was best. The paradigm of engaging interdependently with other adults around issues of improved student learning was not yet in my line of vision. But it soon would be.

You might wonder whether you are actually prepared and ready to lead your colleagues to take action toward a vision that aspires to remove faculty and administrative isolation as a norm. You are. From classroom teaching experiences, you know students learn best when working together and communicating around meaningful work. It should seem natural to you that adults will, too. Joining or becoming a *learning organization* requires you to fully engage in discussion and dialogue with your lateral E-W colleagues on your faculty or administrative learning teams.

The idea of learning and growing together—solving problems as a team—has become an evolving movement. In a broader sense, the idea of learning communities is at the core of the attempt to define a culture of professionalism and on-site professional development in education. In the literature, *learning organizations*, *organizational learning*, *learning communities*, and *professional communities for learning* are all phrases that emerged to describe a school culture striving to become a learning institution. What attracts us to pursue PLCs as a movement is their ability to build adult knowledge and skill capacity and empower every teacher and school leader to improve student learning.

In 1998, *Professional Learning Communities at Work* by Richard DuFour and Robert Eaker captured the summative phrase *professional learning communities*, and the birth of PLCs as a school reform movement began. Convinced that the lack of teacher collaboration and interdependence was less about intent and more about the lack of other models of practice, in *PLCs at Work* DuFour and Eaker described a vision of school organizations as learning institutions for the students and adults, supported by research connected to improved student learning.

In my school district—Stevenson HSD 125—we were fast becoming a model for the movement, without really knowing it at the time. We were beating the path as we walked it. Our school leadership, faculty, and staff entered the new millennium understanding the impact our growth mindset was having on our school community, but not yet fully realizing the dynamics of change required to work in transparent and authentic collaboration with one another. Learning communities of adults have a different psychology than learning communities of students, and are somewhat more complex even though many of the implementation dynamics are the same. Although we had a lot to still learn, there was no turning back. PLCs had become a *movement* in our school district.

In 2005, Mike Schmoker indicated there was an iron-clad case for professional learning communities that "represented the richest most unprecedented culmination of the best we know about authentic school improvement" (p. 136). He cited no less than thirty well-researched and well-respected thought leaders on the topic—from Richard Elmore to Linda Darling-Hammond to Judith Warren Little. As I read his claim for the iron-clad case, I thought, so organizing schools as professional learning communities has become a national movement. Hmm. My next thought was, what is a movement, exactly?

De Pree (1997) indicates there comes a point when exceptional organizations become a movement. He defines a movement as "a collective state of mind, a public and common understanding that the future can be created, not simply experienced or endured" (p. 22). PLCs are, if anything, about creating a hope-filled future. Your life as a school leader is not something just to endure. Your life as a PLC leader provides an opportunity for you to experience your work at its most high-energy, in-the-flow, Quadrant I best. Can your school organization and your school leadership team intentionally shape themselves into the PLC growth mindset of an all-students and all-adults learning *movement?* Yes, and it will take disciplined and well-prepared leaders—lots of them, at all levels of the school organization.

Is there a values and actions litmus test you could apply to determine whether or not your school organization is becoming part of the PLC movement? Yes. I present ten criteria for you to consider. You can use this list as a brief audit to determine how far you are progressing along the PLC road for your specific area of school leadership. (Visit **go.solution-tree.com/plcbooks** to download the *PLC Movement Values and Actions Survey* based on these criteria.)

1. *Common core values* of the shared vision rather than forced rules and regulations dominate decision making.

2. *Fidelity of content and substance* are favored over trivial and superficial team activities.

3. There exists a *sense of urgency* among all adults regarding improving student achievement and closing gaps.

4. Every team and everyone are held *accountable to the results* of their work.

5. There is a high *relational and technical competence* among the majority of the adults.

6. Tensions within the PLC work are balanced by and immersed in *high levels of trust* among the adults.

7. *Constructive conflict is expected* and embraced as part of the work of the team.

8. There is a *rhythm of innovation and creativity* that brings continued renewal and focused risk taking to the work of the school.

9. There is a *perpetual disquiet with the status quo* and a pursuit to make things better—forever.

10. *Uplifting leaders* enable, enrich, and energize the district, the school, or the program area of their school leadership.

These ten characteristics hint at the outcomes of our study and work in this leadership book. What is it about the leadership within a PLC that makes a distinctive difference in the development and pursuit of these cultural elements? As a PLC leader, what must you be *really good at* in order to improve on the school culture, have a deep impact on student and adult learning, and run the PLC leadership race well? These are questions I have tried to answer in this book. Becoming an effective leader starts with understanding the role you play in either creating or closing the knowing-doing gap of those in your sphere of influence. That is, even if fellow administrators, faculty, and staff *know* they should collaborate and work together around issues of improved student learning, why would some choose not to *do* it? And why would you, as a PLC leader, tolerate adult behaviors inconsistent with these PLC vision aspirations?

Becoming an effective leader ends with understanding that your pursuit to close these aspiration gaps will never end. These PLC leadership disciplines become part of your intentional way of living and leading. The training is not something you can do one time and be done. And I know it is hard. It has been a lifelong struggle for me to determine how to lead really well, *every day.* It is a lifelong process and pursuit for you, too. You may read and reread parts of this book from time to time. No matter how good or bad your school story is today, it will be better five years from now if you follow these five leadership disciplines. You might want to choose one discipline and become really good at it. Maybe that discipline is accountability and celebration (turning vision into action), or maybe for the current stage of your leadership career it is reflection and balance (full engagement and energy in your work). Regardless of which discipline you choose, you will be more than ready to defeat the external forces that invariably try to cause your district, school, or area of school leadership to drift.

I would love to hear from you about the book, your reaction to its guidance, and your own personal PLC leadership journey. Did the book connect to your work life? Did the disciplines connect to you personally? If so, which one of the five disciplines was most relevant for you? Did the book allow for positive and robust discussions within your leadership or teacher team? With those in your N-S-E-W sphere? Were the study guides helpful? Did I miss something? From your leadership point of view, are there other leadership struggles you encounter that are not addressed by the five disciplines in this book? You can make comments about the book at tkanold.blogspot.com or at twitter.com using #plcleaders, or follow me at twitter.com/tkanold. I wish you well in your PLC leadership journey!

# References and Resources

Adlai E. Stevenson High School. (2010). *District 125 vision statement for Stevenson High School.* Accessed at www.d125.org/about/district_125_board_of _education_vision_statement.aspx on December 3, 2010.

All Things PLC. (2011). *All things PLC, all in one place.* Accessed at www.allthingsplc .info/ on May 23, 2011.

Amabile, T., & Kramer, S. (2010). What really motivates workers. *The HBR list: Breakthrough ideas for 2010.* Cambridge, MA: Harvard Business School. Accessed at http://hbr.org/2010/01/the-hbr-list-breakthrough-ideas-for-2010 /ar/1 on July 5, 2010.

Barth, R. S. (2001). *Learning by heart.* San Francisco: Jossey-Bass.

Block, P. (1993). *Stewardship: Choosing service over self-interest.* San Francisco: Berrett-Koehler.

Burns, J. M. (1978). *Leadership.* New York: Harper & Row.

Carroll, L. (1955). *Alice in Wonderland.* Racine, WI: Whitman.

Collins, J. (2001). *Good to great: Why some companies make the leap . . . and others don't.* New York: HarperCollins.

Collins, J. (2005). *Good to great and the social sectors: A monograph to accompany* Good to great. New York: HarperCollins.

Collins, J. (2009). *How the mighty fall: And why some companies never give in.* New York: HarperCollins.

Collins, J., & Porras, J. (1997). *Built to last.* New York: HarperCollins.

Conzemius, A., & O'Neill, J. (2002). *The handbook for SMART school teams.* Bloomington, IN: Solution Tree Press.

Covey, S. M. R. (2006). *The speed of trust: The one thing that changes everything.* New York: Free Press.

Crystal, B., & Smith, I. (Producers) & Underwood, R. (Director). (1991). *City slickers* [Motion picture]. United States: Castle Rock Entertainment.

Csikszentmihalyi, M. (2002). *Flow: The classic work on how to achieve happiness.* New York: Harper & Row.

Csikszentmihalyi, M. (2008). *Flow: The psychology of optimal experience.* New York: Harper & Row.

Darling-Hammond, L., & Richardson, N. (2009). Teacher learning: What matters? *Educational Leadership, 66*(5), 46–53.

Deal, T., & Key, M. K. (1998). *Corporate celebration: Play, purpose, and profit at work.* San Francisco: Berrett-Koehler.

Deal, T., & Peterson, K. (1999). *Shaping school culture: The heart of leadership.* San Francisco: Jossey-Bass.

De Pree, M. (1989). *Leadership is an art.* New York: Doubleday.

De Pree, M. (1997). *Leading without power: Finding hope in serving community.* San Francisco: Jossey-Bass.

Deresiewicz, W. (2010). Solitude and leadership. *The American Scholar.* Accessed at www.theamericanscholar.org/solitude-and-leadership/ on June 3, 2010.

Drath, W. (1998). Approaching the future of leadership development. In C. McCauley (Ed.), *The Center for Creative Leadership handbook of leadership development* (pp. 403–432). San Francisco: Jossey-Bass.

Drath, W. (2001). *The deep blue sea: Rethinking the sources of leadership.* San Francisco: Jossey-Bass.

Drath, W. (2008). Issues & observations: Leadership beyond leaders and followers. *Leadership in Action, 28*(5), 20–24.

DuFour, R., DuFour, R., & Eaker, R. (2008). *Revisiting professional learning communities at work: New insights for improving schools.* Bloomington, IN: Solution Tree Press.

DuFour, R., DuFour, R., Eaker, R., & Many, T. (2006). *Learning by doing: A handbook for professional learning communities at work.* Bloomington, IN: Solution Tree Press.

DuFour, R., & Eaker, R. (1998). *Professional learning communities at work: Best practices for enhancing student achievement.* Bloomington, IN: Solution Tree Press.

DuFour, R., & Marzano, R. J. (2011). *Leaders of learning: How district, school, and classroom leaders improve student achievement.* Bloomington, IN: Solution Tree Press.

Dweck, C. S. (2006). *Mindset: The new psychology of success.* New York: Random House.

Education Commission of the States. (2010). *Accountability.* Accessed at http://www.ecs.org/html/issue.asp?issueid=2&subissueID=0 on March 16, 2010.

Frick, D. M., & Spears, L. C. (Eds.). (1996). *On becoming a servant leader: The private writings of Robert Greenleaf.* San Francisco: Jossey-Bass.

Fullan, M. (2001). *Leading in a culture of change.* San Francisco: Jossey-Bass.

Fullan, M. (2008). *The six secrets of change: What the best leaders do to help their organizations survive and thrive.* San Francisco: Jossey-Bass.

Gallimore, R., Ermeling, B. A., Saunders, W. M., & Goldenberg, C. (2009). Moving the learning of teaching closer to practice: Teacher education implications of school-based inquiry teams. *Elementary School Journal, 109*(5), 537–553.

Gardner, J. (1969). *No easy victories.* New York: HarperCollins.

Gardner, J. (1988). *The changing nature of leadership.* Washington, DC: Leadership Studies Program, Independent Sector.

Gardner, J. (1990). *On leadership.* New York: Free Press.

Gardner, J. (1992). The secret ailment. *Across the Board, 12*(8), 41–43.

Gardner, J., Gardner, F., & Moyers, B. (2003). *Living, leading, and the American dream.* San Francisco: Jossey-Bass.

Garmston, R. J., & Wellman, B. M. (2008). *The adaptive school: A sourcebook for developing collaborative groups* (2nd ed.). Boston: Christopher-Gordon.

Gleick, J. (2000). *Faster: The acceleration of just about everything.* New York: Vintage. Accessed at www.fasterbook.com on June 23, 2010.

Goffee, R., & Jones, G. (2006). *Why should anyone be led by you? What it takes to be an authentic leader.* Boston: Harvard Business School Press.

Goleman, D. (2001). An EI-based theory of performance. In C. Chernis & D. Goleman (Eds.), *The emotionally intelligent workplace* (pp. 27–44). San Francisco: Jossey-Bass.

Goleman, D. (2005). *Emotional intelligence: Why it can matter more than IQ.* New York: Bantam Books.

Goleman, D. (2007). *Social intelligence: The new science of human relationships.* New York: Bantam Books.

Goleman, D., Boyatzis, R., & McKee, A. (2002). *Primal leadership: Realizing the power of emotional intelligence.* Boston: Harvard Business School Press.

GoodReads. (2010). *Søren Kierkegaard quotes.* Accessed at www.goodreads.com /author/quotes/6172.S_ren_Kierkegaard on June 6, 2010.

Hock, D. (2000). The art of chaordic leadership. *Leader to Leader Journal, 15*, 20–26.

Kanold, T. (2002). *The power of a learning community: Implications for leadership practices and beliefs in a learning organization.* Ann Arbor, MI: UMI Services.

Kanold, T. (2006). The flywheel effect: Educators gain momentum from a model for continuous improvement. *Journal of Staff Development, 27*(2), 16–21.

Katzenbach, J. R., & Smith, D. K. (1993). *The wisdom of teams: Creating the high-performance organization.* Boston: Harvard Business School Press.

King Rice, J. (2010). *Principal effectiveness and leadership in an era of accountability: What research says.* Urban Institute. Accessed at www.urban.org/publications /1001370.html on April 8, 2010.

Kotter, J. P. (1999). *John P. Kotter on what leaders really do.* Boston: Harvard Business School Press.

Kotter, J., & Whitehead, L. (2010). *Buy-in: Saving your good idea from getting shot down.* Boston: Harvard Business Review Press.

Kouzes, J., & Posner, B. (1999). *Encouraging the heart: A leader's guide to rewarding and recognizing others.* San Francisco: Jossey-Bass.

Kouzes, J., & Posner, B. (2006). *A leader's legacy.* San Francisco: Jossey-Bass.

Little, J. W., & Bartlett, L. (2010). The teacher workforce and problems of educational equity. *Review of Research in Education, 34*(1), 285–328.

Loehr, J. (2007). *The power of story: Change your story, change your destiny in business and in life.* New York: Free Press.

Loehr, J., & Schwartz, T. (2003). *The power of full engagement: Managing energy, not time, is the key to high performance.* New York: Free Press.

Marzano, R. (2007). *The art and science of teaching: A comprehensive framework for effective instruction.* Alexandria, VA: Association for Supervision and Curriculum Development.

Marzano, R., & Pickering, D. (2011). *The highly engaged classroom.* Bloomington, IN: Marzano Research Laboratory.

Marzano, R., & Waters, T. (2009). *District leadership that works: Striking the right balance.* Bloomington, IN: Solution Tree Press.

McArdle, W., Katch, F. I., & Katch, V. L. (2007). *Exercise physiology: Energy, nutrition, and human performance* (6th ed.). Philadelphia: Lippincott Williams & Wilkins.

McFedries, P. (2010). Hurry sickness. *Word spy.* Accessed at www.wordspy.com/words /hurrysickness.asp on May 7, 2010.

Morgan, G. (1997). *Images of organization* (2nd ed.). Thousand Oaks, CA: SAGE.

Muhammad, A. (2009). *Transforming school culture: How to overcome staff division.* Bloomington, IN: Solution Tree Press.

Munger, L., & von Frank, V. (2010). *Change, lead, succeed: Building capacity with school leadership teams.* Oxford, OH: National Staff Development Council.

Noguera, P. A. (2004). Transforming high schools. *Educational Leadership, 61*(8), 26–31.

Patterson, K., Grenny, J., Maxfield, D., McMillan, R., & Switzler, A. (2008). *Influencer: The power to change anything.* New York: McGraw-Hill.

Peters, T. J., & Waterman, R. H., Jr. (1982). *In search of excellence: Lessons from America's best-run companies.* New York: Warner Books.

Pfeffer, J., & Sutton, R. I. (2000). *The knowing-doing gap: How smart companies turn knowledge into action.* Boston: Harvard Business School Press.

Pfeffer, J., & Sutton, R. I. (2006). *Hard facts, dangerous half-truths, and total nonsense: Profiting from evidence-based management.* Boston: Harvard Business School Press.

Pink, D. (2009). *Drive: The surprising truth about what motivates us.* New York: Riverhead.

Quinn, R. E. (2004). *Building the bridge as you walk on it: A guide for leading change.* San Francisco: Jossey-Bass.

Rath, T., & Conchie, B. (2008). *Strengths based leadership: Great leaders, teams, and why people follow.* New York: Gallup Press.

Reeves, D. (2006). *The learning leader: How to focus school improvement for better results.* Alexandria, VA: Association for Supervision and Curriculum Development.

Richardson, J. (2005). Transform your group into a team. *Tools for Schools, 9*(2), 1–2.

Sagie, A., Zaidman, N., Amichai-Hamburger, Y., Te'eni, D., & Schwartz, D. G. (2002). An empirical assessment of the loose-tight leadership model: Quantitative and qualitative analysis. *Journal for Organizational Behavior, 23*(3), 303–320.

Saphier, J. (2005). Masters of motivation. In R. DuFour, R. Eaker, & R. DuFour (Eds.), *On common ground: The power of professional learning communities* (pp. 85–113). Bloomington, IN: Solution Tree Press.

Schmoker, M. (1999). *Results: The key to continuous school improvement* (2nd ed.). Alexandria, VA: Association for Supervision and Curriculum Development.

Schmoker, M. (2005). Here and now: Improving teaching and learning In R. DuFour, R. Eaker, & R. DuFour (Eds.), *On common ground: The power of professional learning communities* (pp. xi–xvi). Bloomington, IN: Solution Tree Press.

Schwartz, T. (2010). *The way we're working isn't working: The four forgotten needs that energize great performance.* New York: Free Press.

Scott, S. (2011). *Fierce leadership: A bold alternative to the worst best practices of business today.* New York: Crown Business.

Senge, P. (1990). *The fifth discipline: The art and practice of the learning organization.* New York: Currency.

Senge, P., Kleiner, A., Roberts, C., Ross, R., Roth, G., & Smith, B. (1999). *The dance of change: The challenges to sustaining momentum in learning organizations.* New York: Doubleday/Currency.

Sergiovanni, T. J. (1992). *Moral leadership: Getting to the heart of school improvement.* San Francisco: Jossey-Bass.

Sergiovanni, T. J. (2005). *Strengthening the heartbeat: Leading and learning together in schools.* San Francisco: Jossey-Bass.

Shaw, G. B. (1903). *Man and superman: A comedy and a philosophy.* New York: Penguin Classics.

Sowder, J. T. (2007). The mathematics education and development of teachers. In F. K. Lester Jr. (Ed.), *Second handbook of research on mathematics teaching and learning* (pp. 186–215). Reston, VA: National Council of Teachers of Mathematics.

Sparks, D. (2005). Leading for transformation in teaching, learning, and relationships. In R. DuFour, R. Eaker, & R. DuFour (Eds.), *On common ground: The power of professional learning communities* (pp. 155–175). Bloomington, IN: Solution Tree Press.

Sullivan, P. (2010). *Clutch: Why some people excel under pressure and others don't.* New York: Penguin.

Tichy, N. (1997). *The leadership engine: How winning companies build leaders at every level.* New York: HarperBusiness.

Tichy, N. (2002). *The cycle of leadership: How great leaders teach their companies to win.* New York: HarperBusiness.

Tichy, N., & Bennis, W. G. (2007). *Judgment: How winning leaders make great calls.* New York: Portfolio.

# Index

■ ■ ■ ■ ■

### Leaders of Learning
*Richard DuFour and Robert J. Marzano*
Together, DuFour and Marzano focus on district leadership, principal leadership, and team leadership, and address how individual teachers can be most effective in leading students—by learning with colleagues how to implement the most promising pedagogy in their classrooms.
**BKF455**

### Becoming an Authentic Learning Leader: Whatever You Do, Inspire Me!
*Timothy D. Kanold*
Kanold helps educators reflect on their core beliefs about the importance of leadership within a professional learning community and shows how leaders can use those beliefs to inspire the skeptics, cynics, and rebels. By examining eight fundamental disciplines of inspirational leadership, Kanold provides the support and focus needed to sustain effective leadership over time.
**DVF029**

### A Leader's Companion
*Robert Eaker, Rebecca DuFour, and Richard DuFour*
Treat yourself to daily moments of reflection with inspirational quotes collected from a decade of work by renowned PLC experts. The uplifting wisdom inside this book will fuel your passion to be a leader in your PLC.
**BKF227**

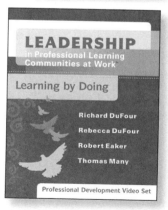

### Leadership in Professional Learning Communities at Work™
*Richard DuFour, Rebecca DuFour, Robert Eaker, and Thomas Many*
Watch leaders in action within a PLC. This short program for PLC leaders uses unscripted interviews and footage from schools to illustrate the role of effective leadership, particularly from the principal, in embedding PLC practices and values in a school.
**DVF024**